THE DRAGON'S PUPILS
A China Odyssey

THE DRAGON'S PUPILS
A China Odyssey

KENNETH STARCK

Iowa State University Press / Ames

KENNETH STARCK is a professor of journalism and director of the University of Iowa School of Journalism and Mass Communication.

FRONTISPIECE: The Great Wall of China, photographed at Mutianyu outside Beijing

All photographs by Kenneth Starck

© 1991 Iowa State University Press, Ames, Iowa 50010
All rights reserved

Manufactured in the United States of America
⊛ This book is printed on acid-free paper.

First edition, 1991

Library of Congress Cataloging-in-Publication Data
Starck, Kenneth.
  The dragon's pupils : a China odyssey / Kenneth Starck. — 1st ed. p.   cm.
  Includes bibliographical references and index.
  ISBN 0-8138-1267-4 (alk. paper)
  1. China — Social life and customs — 1976– 2. China — Politics and government — 1976– 3. Students — China. I. Title.
DS779.23.S73   1991
951.05′8 — dc20   90–47593

畫 龍 點 睛

*Bring the painted dragon to life
by putting in the pupils of the eyes.*

For my Chinese students

CONTENTS

III

IV

FOREWORD

Few subjects in contemporary history are more fascinating or more important than the emergence of the People's Republic of China from centuries of poverty, invasion by foreign powers, colonial occupation, and civil war into one of the most important nations in the world. The need to understand the outcome of this historical process is pressing. The nations of the West cannot afford to ignore the increasingly important political, economic, and social changes that continue to transform the role China plays on the international stage.

Kenneth Starck has written an informative contemporary portrait of the most populous nation in the world. The author is a professor, but this work does not purport to be scholarly; he has sought instead to reach a broad audience. The author is also a journalist, but he does not strive to compete with those colleagues whose work too often is ruled by deadlines and other editorial constraints. Rather, Professor Starck's book is a notable example of cultural reporting at its most perceptive — a careful attempt to describe a foreign culture in its own terms. The genre is a difficult one — not practiced enough by those who write about other nations — because of the constant risk of lapsing conveniently into the habit of refracting another society's experience through Western eyes.

In writing this book, Professor Starck has drawn heavily upon his travels in the People's Republic of China and his experiences with a group of extraordinary young men and women who were his graduate students in journalism at the Chinese Academy of Social Sciences. He would be the first to acknowledge that one year in China is not time enough to master a civilization that is thousands of years old. But it is long enough to observe events, appraise changes, and discern attitudes. When this opportunity is combined with a sensitive eye and a talent for storytelling, the result is a book that broadens our understanding of one of the world's most significant cultures.

When I lectured in Professor Starck's classroom in Beijing in

March 1987, I was deeply impressed by the ambition and perceptiveness of his students. Their command of English was fluent, and their persistent questions about my views on issues of American politics and China's place in international affairs made clear how well Professor Starck had taught them the basic investigative skills and qualities of mind of the journalist's trade.

The students pressed me forcefully about the sincerity of my interest in establishing exchange programs between the University of Iowa and Chinese universities. Could I seriously believe that Chinese universities had something to offer to American students and faculty? They were skeptical of, perhaps startled by, my assertion that the world was on the threshold of what Ambassador Mike Mansfield has called "the Century of the Pacific." Was I merely patronizing them?

One theme is especially clear in Professor Starck's recounting of his year in Beijing: the function of education in building understanding among cultures. It will be talented students like those whose minds were challenged and stretched in Professor Starck's classroom, and who appear so vividly in this book, who will chart China's path into "the Century of the Pacific."

Professor Starck has recounted the pace and impact of the many extraordinary changes occurring in China today. Much of the promise of the revolution that brought Mao Zedong to power in 1949 was tragically crushed during the brutal decade of the Cultural Revolution. But the changes that have occurred under the subsequent leadership of Deng Xiaoping have reached into virtually every aspect of the country's traditional society. Despite the shocking events of Tiananmen Square in June 1989, these changes will not be deterred. China will continue to play a leading role on the world stage, and the changes of the late seventies and eighties still suggest a new promise on the part of the Chinese people to strengthen the capacity of China to be an even more significant force in the political, economic, social, and cultural arenas of the world.

Kenneth Starck has increased our understanding of the profound impact of the transitions that China is experiencing. Perhaps most important of all, he has given impressive testimony of the decisive role that education will play in preparing the young people of the People's Republic of China for the responsibilities of national leadership and world citizenship.

JAMES O. FREEDMAN
President, Dartmouth College

Acknowledgments

Acknowledging without blaming in a cross-cultural venture of this sort is delicate, but I must express personal appreciation to a number of people: William J. Zima, a colleague who first detected promise in articles I had written while in China and then offered valuable advice; Phyllis Fleming of the *Cedar Rapids Gazette,* who suggested that I consider writing articles for her newspaper; Pei-wei Cheng, who got me interested in China; twenty-one extraordinary Chinese students; Shelly Wyffels, an undergraduate scholar assistant who was always willing to check just one more library source; Yu Xu, a Chinese scholar who reviewed the manuscript with a sharp and balanced eye; Chen Yun, for the calligraphy; and those who offered valuable criticisms of various manuscript versions or helped in other ways, including Maynard Cuppy, Vishwas Gaitonde, Larry Johnson, Dean Kruckeberg, Frank Petrella, Nancy Prawdzik, Laurie Rossi, Fran Somers, Sun Changqing, and Gary Whitby. Mary Russell Curran brought a sensitive editorial eye to the manuscript, and Sandra McJimsey oversaw production in a way authors appreciate. Special thanks to my wife, Raija, and daughter, Christa, whose lives not only became part of the book but were affected by it. The Iowa School of Journalism and Mass Communication provided research support through its John F. Murray Fund. For any merit the book may have, I owe a great debt to many people. For any deficiencies, I alone am accountable.

One note about the spelling of Chinese names and other words: I have used the romanized Pinyin system, which differs from earlier romanized versions (such as Wade-Giles and Lessing) of the Chinese script. Though the change to Pinyin began in the late 1950s, it still causes confusion. In Pinyin, Peking becomes Beijing; Tientsin, Tianjin; and Mao Tse-tung, Mao Zedong.

THE DRAGON'S PUPILS
A China Odyssey

PROLOGUE

Even for someone interested in cross-cultural experiences, the opportunity to go to China for a year forces sober reflection. The nation is in the midst of dramatic change. Headlines bearing China datelines often tell of turmoil or tragedy. Black students from Africa protest treatment by Chinese authorities. Chinese students clamor for more democracy and, in Tiananmen Square, are willing to sacrifice their careers and their lives. Buddhists riot in Tibet, where issues of freedom and independence spill into the streets and monasteries, and people die. Calamitous earthquakes and transportation disasters seem to occur with unnatural frequency. Is such bad news all there is? Are our own perceptions skewed? Do Western journalists dwell mainly on the aberrations? The answers, it seems to me, are yes, yes, and yes.

I had been to China once before, for three weeks in the fall of 1984, to give lectures at one of China's premier universities, Fudan, in Shanghai. My initial contact had come about unexpectedly. A Fudan journalism professor, Pei-wei (Bill) Cheng, a few years earlier had sent a letter addressed merely to "director" in care of the University of Iowa School of Journalism and Mass Communication. In the letter he introduced himself as a 1951 M.A. graduate of the school and said he wanted to reestablish ties with his alma mater. Like his country, he was emerging slowly from China's Cultural Revolution (also known as the Great Proletarian Cultural Revolution), a decade-long (1966–1976) campaign launched by Chairman Mao Zedong to rekindle revolutionary fervor and to restore the ideals of the struggle that gave birth in 1949 to modern China. Professor Cheng's wife, Kate, also was an Iowa graduate, in music. During the ten-year nightmare, Professor Cheng had had to work as a cook in the countryside. To avoid trouble from the Red Guards (the more than ten million young people

3

who rallied to Chairman Mao's call for revolution and then committed countless acts of vandalism and murder), Professor Cheng and his wife had disposed of anything that might be associated with elitism and "bourgeois" Westernism. They even had destroyed their Iowa graduation diplomas. After extensive correspondence, we exchanged lecture visits and helped pave the way for an educational exchange program between our universities. We also became close friends. We even negated a small part of the malevolence of the Cultural Revolution by finding the company that prints Iowa graduation certificates and replacing the diplomas.

Later, when the chance came to spend an extended time in China under the Fulbright program, my Finnish-born wife, Raija, and I weighed the prospects. What would happen to careers? Home? Family? What would China be like for an extended period of time? What would our living conditions be? Would there be restrictions on teaching? Would we be able to travel freely? Would we, an American and a Finn, who already had made some cultural accommodations, be able to adjust to this new culture? What about language?

Some of the questions were easy to deal with. In China, we would, after all, be pursuing professional interests. We would rent our Iowa home to a family on sabbatical leave from another institution. Our daughter, seventeen at the time, preferred to spend the academic year as a university student at Iowa and would join us in Beijing in the spring.

Concerns about adjustment and culture were more difficult. We consulted friends and others who had been to China. Their reports, whether they had been tourists or long-term residents, were mixed. Some had disliked the China experience. Others had had a hard time leaving. Soon it became clear to us that the experiences of those we talked to or read about were mostly a reflection of their own personalities and values. What else, after all, could the experiences be but their own interpretations? The meaning of any experience lies within the person. A cross-cultural encounter merely intensifies the experience.

We discovered that for some people, positive expectations of a visit to China had been fulfilled. For others, they had not. Expectations, whatever their source, had varied a great deal. So, then, did individual reactions or perceptions. A two-week traveler on an organized tour, to be sure, brings away impressions quite different from those of the person who spends six or more months living in another culture. China visitors who had come away with a negative experience, who vowed never to return to China, seemed to have drawn cultural parameters for themselves. Or, more accurately, their own culture had determined their boundaries of acceptance and tolerance, both physical and intellectual.

Somewhere between mountains of expectations and perceptions lie the plains of reality. Here is where human beings play out their daily lives. What is the reality of China? What were our expectations before going there? What was the reality of our experience? These questions have prompted this book. The chapters reflect answers filtered through the distinctive cultural lenses that Raija and I brought to the experience.

At the outset, I must say that our year in China was probably the most exhilarating and frustrating of our lives — exhilarating because of the constant mind-expanding experiences, frustrating because of the need to cope with drastically different ways of doing things. What does a Westerner think when told that the distance from one place to another is "Ten *li* if you walk, but five *li* if you run"? (A *li* is a Chinese measure of distance, about one-third of a mile.) What was that again? It is shorter from here to there if you run? The story may be apocryphal, but it does raise fundamental questions about distance and time. Is a day long? Perhaps it makes sense to think of a day or a year — or life — as round.

This scrambling of senses is what takes place when one way of thinking encounters another way of thinking. Experiencing a culture different from our own may lead to a loosening of the straitjacket imposed upon us by our native culture. It permits us to be liberated from our own culture and, as a result, to gain insight into it.

Years ago, a then-young Walter Lippmann, a favorite author among my Chinese students, stated a truism in his classic *Public Opinion* (1922, 54–55): "For the most part we do not first see, and then define, we define first and then see." We still seem to think of perception, though, according to the axiom "Seeing is believing." We ought to recognize as equally valid the notion that believing is seeing.

The lesson is simple yet profound. It suggests that predisposition and stereotype are twin cousins of prejudice and narrow-mindedness. How does one remove cultural impediments? With difficulty. And probably never completely. But at least one ought to be able to recognize that there are different ways of seeing things. Not necessarily true or false or correct or incorrect, but *different*. There *are* different ways of seeing.

Seeing and believing were also at issue fifteen hundred years ago during the Liang dynasty in Nanjing, China. Legend holds that Emperor Liang was enthusiastic about decorating Buddhist temples and often ordered a painter, Zhang, to draw something. At a temple in Nanjing (then Jinlin), Zhang drew four white dragons. He left out the pupils of their eyes. When asked why he did this, Zhang replied, "If I add the pupils, the dragons will instantly fly away." People laughed. They insisted that Zhang put the pupils in the eyes of two of the dragons. He did. Amidst thunder and lightning, the temple walls came tumbling down, and, sure enough, two of the dragons roared off into the blue sky. As for the other two dragons, they are still there—without pupils.

The legend, for me, conveys a double meaning. The pupils of the eyes symbolize experience that gives life to reality. And the word *pupils*, synonymous in the English language to *students*, reminds us that, culturally, we are all "pupils."

This collection of pieces represents a cultural journey—discoveries occurring over the span of a year (1986–1987) and continuing to evolve.

I

一

GRADUATE STUDENTS at the Institute of Journalism of the Chinese Academy of Social Sciences pose with the author in front of the building housing the institute in the eastern part of Beijing.

1 ACADEMIC HAPPINESS

Buoyed by recent change in their lives and prospects for more change in their country, the twenty-one men and women on that early September morning reached out with expressions of warmth, friendliness, and expectancy. Some had seen the Cultural Revolution (1966–1976) intrude senselessly into their young lives. After finishing high school in his hometown of Datong in Shanxi Province, Zeng Lintong, now twenty-eight, had been, as the Chinese euphemistically put it, "sent down to the countryside" for two years of work and ideological reeducation. The work was supposed to build up the nation but often amounted to menial tasks or busywork. The experience, though bitter for Zeng Lintong, had not diminished his aspirations or his sense of humor. Quoting a Chinese proverb, he said, "If you work at it hard enough, you can grind an iron rod into a needle."

As the Cultural Revolution finally led to disillusionment and sadness, Zeng Lintong studied on his own and was admitted to Shanxi University, where he studied English. With a flair for English, he became a translator for a foreign trade office and eventually accompanied a delegation on a brief visit to the United States. He was the only student in my class to have visited the States, although two others had been abroad. Jia Su, also from the coal-mining province of Shanxi, had worked as a translator for a group that made a brief visit to Helsinki, Finland. Another student had been to Paris for a short time as a translator on a United Nations project.

Arriving this day in this starkly plain but adequate classroom had been a challenge for the cheerful Zeng Lintong. Like several of his classmates seeking entry to this journalism studies program, he had not succeeded the first time he took the entrance examinations. Now his life was ready for another career shift. He aspired to become a journalist, and he had some notion of what the profession was all about. "Journalism plays an important role in our society," he said. "Not only can it make us well informed about the whole world, it can impose certain influences on people's lives and even the policy of the government." The last comment — about affecting government policy — reflected future hopes rather than current realities.

Sitting at the front of the classroom, where the seven women in the class always sat, was Xu Yichun, now twenty-nine. She was also old enough to remember how the Cultural Revolution had affected her. At the age of sixteen, she too had responded to the call of Chairman Mao Zedong and had gone to the countryside. She had lived there four years. "Now I can hardly imagine how I passed that time," she reflected, adding with steely resolution, "But I have won."

Xu Yichun was one of four students from Zhejiang Province in east central China. She was eager for this opportunity to pursue a new career. From Hangzhou, she had been teaching English. Her language competency had helped her secure one of the twenty-one slots in this year's journalism class. If other students had not pointed it out, I would not have known Xu Yichun's husband was also in the class. They sat in different rows and lived in separate quarters on the top floor of the four-story building, which quite literally housed the journalism program and those in it. The family arrangements might strike an American as odd, but the nation was experiencing a critical housing shortage, especially in the cities. And these students were not strangers to difficult times. Xu Yichun had a favorite slogan to see her through: "Fight with smile."

The average age of the students was twenty-seven. The oldest was Chang Weimin, thirty-four, from the Ningxia Hui Autonomous Region. He was the father of a one-year-old son and, for now at least, had to live apart from his family. The youngest, a woman and two men, were twenty-one. They had just finished their undergraduate degrees, and this graduate program was the next step for them.

They were all master's students in the Institute of Journalism of the Chinese Academy of Social Sciences (CASS). More than a dozen had already taught English at one time or another in their lives. Now they were taking a major step toward playing important roles in China's future. Their tuition was free, as it still is for all university students, and their expenses were provided primarily by two sponsoring news organizations and their previous "work units" (or, in Chinese, *danwei*). Sixteen eventually would work for Xinhua, the government's domestic and international information agency, often referred to as the New China News Agency; five would join the *China Daily,* the internationally distributed, English-language daily newspaper. For the time being, these organizations would serve as the students' work units.

Everyone working in China is associated with a work unit. Mine was Xinhua. The work unit represents an extended family, a minisociety, with the privileges as well as the controls that accompany such an arrangement. For example, when I purchased a bicycle, I had to have an official statement of approval from Xinhua. When I left the country for a few weeks and returned, I also needed approval. Besides regulating activities, the work unit also sponsored social events and generally provided assistance when called upon.

Our classroom was in a building on the same grounds occupied by the *People's Daily,* the primary organ of the Communist party, and the *China Daily.* Surrounding the compound—as such complexes are commonly called—were the usual fence and, in some places, a wall. The barriers here and elsewhere seemed to represent a contradiction: the protection of privacy in the otherwise public nature of life in China. The plain concrete buildings were rectangular and must have had an aged look even at the time of completion. The best thing about the compound was that it was set in a pleasant, campuslike atmosphere. There were trees and grass and sidewalks, as well as an outdoor basketball court that doubled as a soccer field.

The students and I were about to spend a year together. Our routine would be to meet Monday and Wednesday mornings from 8:30 to 11:30 and to hold individual conferences in the afternoons. Instruction was in English because they had been chosen to work as international journalists—editors, reporters, foreign correspondents, or translators—and English-language competency was one of the foremost requisites.

Our classroom was on the third floor. The second floor housed a journalism research institute, and the first floor was administration. Students lived in Spartan, dormitory-style accommodations on the fourth floor. The living quarters, two to four students to an area, had been fashioned out of several spacious rooms, with blankets and other hangings serving as partitions. Privacy was minimal. But each area had beds, lamps, and desks and had been personalized with family photos and decorations. One student, who had taught English to Chinese soldiers, displayed pictures of tanks and other military weapons.

Eight of the students were married. Five were parents who all had sons. Most had to live apart from their families. One of the more fortunate was Zhao Shengwei, thirty-one, a former teacher from the archipelago of Zhoushan in Zhejiang. His wife and two-year-old son lived on the other side of town, not far from where I lived. When he visited them on weekends, the bus ride took two hours one way. For me, the trip by taxi took less than an hour.

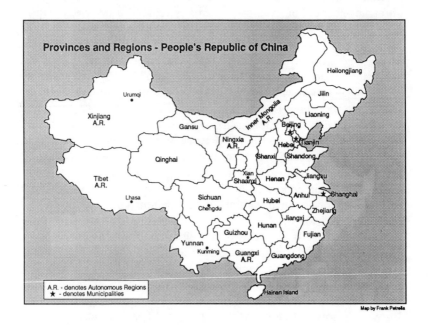

Map by Frank Petrella

The students came from all over China but mostly from the central southern region. They represented nine different provinces, from Guangxi in the south to Jilin in the north. Four came from Anhui Province and four from Zhejiang Province.

As a group, the students would spoil me with their infectious enthusiasm. Seldom have I experienced such personal satisfaction in the classroom. Of course, I learned as much as they did—from them as individuals and from their reporting assignments, which they carried out on the manual typewriters provided by the work units. Over the period of a year, I was allowed a glimpse into their lives and could see determination, sacrifice, hardship, aspiration, frustration. Through their eyes I was given a view of China not afforded many visitors.

They could have been any group of graduate students anywhere — bright, eager, and industrious — but there was a critical difference. This was China, and the debilitating and disastrous change wrought by the Cultural Revolution had suddenly blossomed into other kinds of changes — mostly economic, so far, but some social and, to a lesser degree, political. Personal lives were again being deeply affected. Some skeptics, both inside and outside China, are still wary — and perhaps weary — of the change. They point to centuries of unfulfilled promises for China and believe the change is an illusion. Others disagree, including the many Chinese who find themselves motivated and even prosperous, at least by Chinese standards.

My students interviewed many independent merchants, ranging from cobblers to tailors and from bike repairmen to poultry vendors, and found enthusiastic support for economic reforms. One clothing store operator said that private business is a way of making money, and "I need more money to make financial preparations for my two sons' marriages." A twenty-eight-year-old independent photography studio operator spoke also about the improved standard of living for the Chinese people and argued that free enterprise was an immediate necessity. "As a theory, private enterprise is opposed to Marxism," he said. "But in China at this stage, we need all sorts of forms of production."

The Chinese like to say they are building socialism "with Chinese characteristics." The move toward an entrepreneurial system was initiated and fostered by Deng Xiaoping, the venerable leader who observed his eighty-fourth birthday in 1988. The economic changes are not without strong internal critics, however, and the fear is that a system of commercial values will creep in.

My own students, though enamored with the West, especially with most things American, often expressed concern about foreign influences on the "spiritual" side of Chinese life. They were not making a religious statement: they were talking about the loosening of family ties and the placing of individual self-interest above community interest.

For overseas firms interested in getting a foothold in China through "joint ventures," the prospect of a billion people as customers was mind-boggling. Changes in the market economy were bringing change everywhere. Friends, "old China hands" who keep returning, expressed amazement at the changes they had seen after being gone just a year or two. But what was taking place in China was not easily understood. Contradictions in government actions abounded. Social and personal tensions traceable to the repressive period of the Cultural Revolution constantly surfaced. And outsiders have their own limits, imposed by their own culture, when trying to fathom what is taking place. Rather than change, perhaps stuttering evolution might be a better description of what was occurring. For, short of outright revolution, structural change in society tends to come slowly, unevenly, and maybe not at all.

For me, China offered unique opportunities to teach, conduct research, and write. As a scholar, I found a social laboratory where theory and practice set off sparks daily. As a journalist, I had countless story possibilities, although admittedly, as John Burns of the *New York Times* found out just before I arrived in Beijing, certain restrictions still hold. (Burns was ordered out of China in 1986, ostensibly for traveling into a restricted area; the expulsion was seen by U.S. diplomats as a reminder to foreign correspondents in China that there are limits to acceptable reporting.)

While students were adjusting to their new lives, my wife and I were doing the same. We began settling into our new home, two spacious rooms with a Western-style toilet in the hospitable Friendship Hotel in the north of Beijing, the capital city that many Westerners still call Peking. The hotel, built in the 1950s to house Soviet advisers, now is used primarily to house foreign experts and tourists. It covers a square block and has nine main buildings, including five dining halls, an outdoor Olympic-size swimming pool, outdoor tennis courts, a barber shop, a medical clinic, and several other shops. It is a self-contained community surrounded by a high fence with two entrances. To some, the place has a disquieting effect because of the way it is separated from everything else. Indeed, the hotel, with its pleasant gardens, walking paths, and children's playgrounds, tends to shield residents from city life. A shy person could become accustomed to these comforts and avoid encounters with the real Beijing. Hotel residents could enter and exit at will. Chinese visitors had to check in at the main entrance gate unless accompanied by a hotel guest.

Our rooms had everything we needed and then some: beds, linens, closets, hot and cold water when we wanted it, a color television, a telephone, mail delivery every day of the week, air conditioning, laundry service, and, perhaps best of all, a window and balcony that looked out to Beijing's Western Hills. It also had a few things we did not need: ten-foot-high ceilings, occasional roaches, constant static on local (but not long-distance) telephone calls, and a panoramic view of the smog that obscured the Western Hills more than half the time. We did not have a kitchen. We could have moved into a unit with a kitchen but did not want to contend with the constant shopping, cooking odors, and food storage problems. Instead, we ate most of our meals in the dining hall designated for foreign experts. The conversation was usually better than the food, and the food itself was generally good.

Most Chinese work units that hire experts from other countries have their own foreign experts office, whose staff members arrange activities for visitors. At the Friendship Hotel, the staff could not have been more accommodating. The foreign experts office organized frequent excursions to cultural events and places of interest throughout the city, region, and country. Hotel services included a daily bus for guests wanting to go to downtown Beijing. The ride went past the Forbidden City and ended at the main Friendship Store, a huge department store for tourists and foreign experts. Here you could buy everything, much of it imported, from clothing to film, liquor to souvenirs, bikes to croissants. Again, Chinese people were not permitted to enter unless accompanied by a foreigner. This kind of special treatment was a source of antagonism to some Chinese and an embarrassment to many visitors.

The sights of Beijing are fascinating, from bustling open markets — there was one just across the street from the hotel — to kite flying in Tiananmen Square to the narrow *hutongs* (residential alleyways) in the old parts of town. Beijing woos you in the fall, the most popular time for tourists. The golden hues of autumn decorate the Forbidden City and the Great Wall in imperial splendor. The winter chill and spring dust we had been warned about did not concern us for now. Beijing is also, of course, the driver's seat of China. Here foreign heads of state begin their visits: Japan's Nakasone, Italy's Craxi, Iceland's Hermannsson, East Germany's Honaker, Britain's Queen Elizabeth. All visited Chinese leaders during just one two-week period in the fall of 1986.

Transportation in a city of nine million inhabitants is a challenge for anyone, let alone a foreigner with a summer's worth of Chinese language studies. The easiest and most enjoyable way for us to travel was by bicycle. Unofficially there were 5,000,002 bikes in Beijing. The last two were my Phoenix and my wife's Flying Pigeon. Easy to bike to were the city's popular tourist attractions, such as the Forbidden City, the Temple of Heaven, Tiananmen Square, Beihai Park, the Summer Palace, and the Beijing Zoo, where Lele was born during our stay (Lele is the world's first second-generation panda conceived through artificial insemination). A little farther out were the Great Wall and the Ming tombs.

In the fall, the city had a number of significant celebrations. There was the fiftieth anniversary of the Long March, a six-thousand-mile trek across mountains, rivers, and swamps by Chairman Mao and his followers. The father of one of my students had made that legendary march and now lived in retirement in Wuhan. The March, dramatically chronicled by Harrison Salisbury in *The Long March: The Untold Story* (1987), has come to symbolize China's struggle for independence.

On October 1, 1986, China observed the thirty-seventh anniversary of its founding. An estimated five million of us crowded into Tiananmen Square for the celebration.

One surprise was the number of American visitors, including Iowans, we encountered. One Sunday morning that fall we spied a University of Iowa colleague, Chinese history professor R. David Arkush, among throngs of people on Wangfujing, one of Beijing's busiest shopping streets. Our six-foot-plus frames helped us recognize one another. In late September at our hotel, we encountered an Iowa City/Cedar Rapids trade mission delegation touring China. Later, a group interested in the work Herbert Hoover had carried out in China visited. They were members of the Herbert Hoover Presidential Library Association. Professional colleagues from Wisconsin, Arizona, Texas, and elsewhere were constantly shuttling in and out.

My primary professional and academic interest, of course, was journalism. With the belief that a nation's communication system is central to everything else in the society and an awareness of the great changes taking place in China, I wanted to learn whether journalism was being affected and, if so, how. I found that reforms in this sector have not kept pace with economic and political reforms. There is much discussion about the appropriate role of the press in emerging China but little consensus. My colleagues at the Department of Journalism met often to discuss what the role of the Chinese press should be. They left exasperated and frustrated, only to return the following week and resume the discussion.

As much as any other sector of society in China today, the press mirrors the stresses of change. It is held tightly under the thumb of the Communist party. But leaders, some at least, believe that more information and more open communication are key ingredients for continued growth and development.

Since the opening of China in the late 1970s, the government has kept at least one eye on the press and its role. As early as 1980, suggestions were made for press reforms through a new press law. Any reforms in the relationship between the government and the press, however, will require fundamental political change.

Journalists themselves do not agree on what the role of the press in "new China" should be. Some believe journalists should have more decision-making authority. There is growing support for the idea that the press function ought to include presentation of news and information, differing viewpoints, entertainment, and advertising. Some say that freedom of speech and publication is a basic condition for political democracy. How that is to be interpreted and implemented is the stumbling block. The changes unleashing free markets in goods and capital have not produced a free market of ideas.

At times, as the pages that follow will show, I was not always sure what I was teaching. At the beginning, I had a clear idea. But as the wave of student demonstrations came on, as repercussions of these events reverberated throughout Chinese society, and as anxieties mounted in the face of classroom restrictions (for example, a prohibition on Western journalists' visiting my classes), I became less certain about what I was teaching. Journalistic writing? Interviewing skills? English usage? Critical thinking? Western ways? Yes, probably all those things and more. Yet, oddly, this apparent ambiguity of purpose did not detract from the experience. Admittedly, toward the end of the year, the classroom atmosphere bordered on stagnation, but students continued to be excited about learning. And sustaining me was the simple wonder of China—its future clinging to its past, as well as its geographic variety and splendor and its enormous potential to improve the lives of its billion-plus citizens, one-fifth of the world's population.

For me it was a never-ending learning experience. By the end of the year, my students had learned enough to realize that this *waiguoren* (foreigner) had one set of expectations of them; Chinese society, another. Their assignments reflected the Janus-like tugs the students experienced. Besides grammar and language usage, I evaluated student work for its completeness, accuracy, and logical—by Western standards, at least—interpretation. Since students were encouraged to submit their work to editors for possible publication, they discovered that my criteria in the classroom were not primary criteria for acceptance by editors. Appropriateness of topic and particular story approach or emphasis were more important in the newsroom.

On that first day of classes, I entered the building through the *People's Daily* compound. An armed guard was at the gate. As I strolled to the journalism building, I passed another guard, with a rifle slung over his right shoulder. Nothing too unusual about this, I was told later. The *People's Daily,* along with other key governmental organizations, is guarded by armed police. Still, armed guards make you think differently about the power of the press.

Near the end of our first month together, I asked students to evaluate, anonymously, the course and to offer suggestions and criticisms. One student, obviously thinking of our pressure-packed writing assignments as well as of the joy of learning, wrote: "It is quite a paradox that I should feel tired with a kind of academic happiness."

The year seemingly could not have begun better. Unknown to us at the time, students on some of the nation's campuses were preparing to lead the charge for more and faster change. But that was several months away. For now, there were other discoveries to be made.

2 BIKE KINGDOM

Past the White Peacock Art World, along the canal paralleling Beijing's second ring road, around the bend right onto south Dongzhimen, and suddenly a green-clad officer looms ahead, left hand extended, palm outward, in body language unmistakable: Stop. Our Phoenix and Flying Pigeon flutter to a halt. Raija and I are bicycling the wrong way on a one-way path. We are trying a shortcut. We have violated the law and are ready to plead guilty, have our bikes confiscated, beg for mercy, and settle for anything less than labor camp.

As people begin gathering to witness the plight of these "big noses" or "tall noses," as Chinese frequently refer to Westerners, the officer asks for something. We are not sure what. But I reach, slowly, into a belt pouch and withdraw my passport. The young officer studies it, scrutinizing the thumb-size photo, comparing it with the hardened face before him. There is a long, breathless pause. Finally, and happily, the officer opts for mercy. He returns the passport to me and motions us back into the direction we came from.

It was just a routine event in the life of a bike rider in Beijing. Make that "Bike-jing." Every day ushers in the Great Bicycle Race. The city is reputed to be the bike capital of the world. China itself might claim the international title as the "kingdom of bikes." People's transportation, they call it with good reason. There are as many bicycles in China as there are people in the United States. Except for chopsticks, bikes may be the most egalitarian feature of the nation's sociopolitical system. In China, bikes and biking tell much about human behavior and social change.

Bikes are as essential to China as cars are to industrialized nations. While biking is a leisure-time activity in some nations, it represents appropriate technology for others, including China. Bikes are

BEIJING CYCLISTS pass by the entrance to the Forbidden City in Tiananmen Square.

relatively inexpensive and pollution-free. Pedal power in China transports just about anything—from family to furniture, from market goods to construction materials. One day the *China Daily* carried a story about two men who robbed a store in south China and managed to get away on a bicycle.

China's bike statistics are enough to make the legs ache: five hundred million bike riders throughout China, five to six million bikes in Beijing, three hundred bike factories, and, finally, thirty-two million bikes manufactured a year (still a million or so short of demand).

Some statistics are frightening: 60 to 70 percent of road accidents involve bikes, and 30 percent of the fatalities are cyclists. In 1985 China had 222,000 traffic accidents, injuring 186,000 persons, 42,000 fatally. Most injuries and deaths occur when trucks, cars, and, occasionally, trains collide with bicyclists. There are legal rights-of-way, of course, but practically speaking right-of-way is defined by size. Astride a bike, one had best not think about accidents too much. I saw bicycles crushed under the tires of heavy-duty trucks and lying crumpled in the middle of the road. I was on a train that killed a cyclist at a crossing. I saw an elderly man haplessly ram his bicycle into a jeep truck that suddenly took a sharp turn. On average I saw one such accident a week.

Despite the dangers, most long-term residents join the bike parade. Bikes offer cheap and convenient transportation, as well as exercise. Best of all, for visitors, at least, traveling around on a bike offers a unique perspective of the land and its people. There is a sense of social involvement and intimacy that one probably cannot get any other way.

By Chinese standards, a bicycle is not cheap. A new name-brand bike, such as Forever or Flying Pigeon, costs about fifty dollars. The Chinese used to have to wait years to buy a good bike, and coupons from a person's work unit were necessary. But with the lifting of price controls in the era of economic reform, this has changed, although top brands can still be hard to get.

Most Chinese bikes have only one speed. In Beijing kickstands and bells are required, although the bells must be for diversion since nobody pays attention when you ring one. Lights for night riders are nonexistent. Until recently, the color of all bikes was black. Most still are, but other colors are appearing now. A new owner must purchase a one-time license, which costs less than a dollar and does not include a safety inspection.

Oddly, the first thing you do with a new bike is not pedal home. It may fall apart before you arrive. You take it to the nearest repair shop for a general inspection and tightening of bolts and screws. Chinese bike factories seem to assemble parts with glue. It is up to the new owner to see that the bolts are tightened and all the parts intact.

Visitors accustomed to merchants who cater to consumers' desires can have a hard time adjusting to shopping in China. Despite dramatic surges in consumption of goods and services, the notion of consumer advocacy is still in its infancy. Once, while looking for bikes for ourselves, Raija and I overhead a young American student sobbing in the basement of the Xidan Department Store, one of the largest in Beijing.

"But I've already had two from here," she managed to say through the tears. "How do I know this one will be any better?"

She told us that the bike she had purchased a few days ago had fallen apart. She had brought it back, had been given another, and had gone only a short distance on the new bike when it too had broken down. Now, as people gathered around to see the plight of this Westerner displaying emotions naturally and openly, she too was breaking down. She had been in Beijing for only a few days. To cap her initiation, she was missing her first Chinese language lesson. As newcomers ourselves, there was little we could do to help. After suggesting to her that she go to her lesson and return to resolve the bicycle crisis, we left. It would not be the first exasperating cultural clash we would encounter. Nor would we always be mere witnesses.

Though bicycles might need attention immediately when they come from the storeroom, the cost of bike repairs and upkeep is unbelievably low. A tune-up plus a new rear axle at Bicycle Repair Shop No. 3 near the Friendship Hotel cost me just under three dollars.

Bike repair shops, in fact, offer a glimpse into China's changing economy. Such shops were among the early private enterprises permitted under Chinese leader Deng Xiaoping in 1978. Now the shops are more numerous than gasoline stations used to be in the United States. An inner-tube repair costs about fifteen cents. Air, free in some places, costs 1 *fen* (one-fourth cent) per tire at other places.

The owner of Bicycle Repair Shop No. 3, Chen Wanzhong, has made the most of it. He has become a minor celebrity with an annual estimated income about ten times the average 1,000 *yuan* ($270 U.S., or $22.50 a month) received by city residents. The fifty-six-year-old business owner has fourteen apprentices and offers "loaners" to those dropping off their bikes for repair.

Getting around on bikes is easy. Many cities, including Beijing, have clearly marked bike lanes — sometimes wider than those for motorized traffic. The millions of vehicles seem to flow methodically and smoothly, though slowly. When there are no traffic police at intersections, controlled chaos erupts. People on foot and bikes fan out in all directions. They show little inhibition about crowding past others or inserting themselves into waiting lines at whatever points they want. Visitors initially express shock over such behavior. But we quickly realized that if we did not go with the flow we would not go at all. That turns out to be a good maxim for coping in another land. "Drift with the stream," is the way the Chinese put it.

Bicyclists in Beijing enjoy a flat terrain, and the pedaling is almost effortless. From the Friendship Hotel, it is a forty-minute bike ride south and east to the Forbidden City and Tiananmen Square. The Summer Palace takes a half hour. Also within comfortable range are the Peking Man Site, Marco Polo Bridge, the Temple of Heaven, and Fragrant Hills.

Bicyclists can also venture down the crowded little side streets, *hutongs,* where, in contrast to what one finds in high-rise apartment buildings, much of the traditional Chinese life-style still goes on. Elderly men sit outside doorways and talk and smoke. Laundry hangs from clotheslines or branches of trees. Grandmothers stroll with grandchildren. Youngsters in their practical slit pants reveal tiny bottoms while squatting to inspect a newly discovered object on the ground. The piercing smells from public toilets compete with aromas drifting from cooking woks.

Bike parking lots, another example of private enterprise, are all over. Owners have to pay attendants, usually elderly women, two *fen* (one-half cent) for a day, or six *fen* (one and one-half cents) for overnight.

One look at the crowded transportation facilities in Beijing is reason enough to rely on a bike. The first time I rode a bus was when a colleague and I were leaving the institute. The bus looked packed, and I suggested we wait for the next bus. She said, "We're lucky—it's not crowded," and, grabbing my arm, wedged us onto the bus. Each day buses and trolleys transport nearly nine million passengers. At times, it seems everyone wants the same seat. Scarcity of nearly everything except people is a characteristic of the way of life in China. A subway system also links parts of the city.

Taxis are expensive. Taxi drivers, many of them formerly in the People's Liberation Army, are among the highest-paid workers in China. I had plenty of experience riding in taxis, since that was the way I got to and from the classroom in the eastern part of town twice a week. I came to refer to contemporary China as the "taxi dynasty." The drivers themselves display many of the characteristics the Chinese have come to associate with a bourgeois, or capitalist, society: aggressiveness, cheating, and rudeness.

Raija and I had numerous arguments with taxi drivers over fares. On one of my first trips from the Institute of Journalism to the Friendship Hotel, a driver took me on an unofficial tour to the outskirts of town. I wound up paying more than twice the normal fare. At the time I did not know any better. Another time, after I had had an unusually heated argument with a taxi driver over a fare, the driver jumped into his car and sped away, the right rear tire of his car brushing up against the back of my right shoe. Except for dulling the shine, the tire did no damage. I had the driver's identification number and the number on his license plate, and I considered writing a letter of complaint to tourist officials. But then I decided that my own behavior had not been exactly exemplary and wrote it off as another phase in the acculturation process.

But there were exceptions to such behavior. One night about 10 p.m., Raija and I arrived at Shanghai's main railway station and needed to get to Fudan University. A taxi driver delivered us almost to the door of the guest house and wrote out a receipt for the amount of the fare — 3.50 *yuan* (less than $1 U.S.). A few nights before we had paid six times that amount for the same trip. The taxi driver refused my offer of a tip and seemed genuinely pleased that we were pleased.

During the year in China, Raija and I traveled in all kinds of transport. Nothing ever beat the bike. In many cities, bicycles can be rented for a few cents an hour. That is the best way to experience Chinese cities, from Hangzhou to Suzhou, from Hohhot to Guilin.

Will automobiles ever challenge China's bicycle dynasty? Not soon, if ever. The nation does not have a good road system, and most cities are too crowded already. A few individuals do own cars, since private ownership of cars is now permitted in Beijing. The first private auto purchase was by a suburban chicken farmer who bought a car and a light truck for her business in 1983. Today the city has eighteen hundred cars owned by individuals, mostly business persons and celebrities — pop stars, actors, athletes, and painters.

While making concessions to cars, China is gearing up to produce even more bikes. Some are for export. The Shanghai Bicycle Factory, China's largest manufacturer and producer of the Forever model, more than doubled its export of bikes for 1988 to 520,000. The Phoenix is also manufactured in Shanghai, by No. 3 Shanghai Bicycle Factory.

Many bikes have more than utilitarian value to their owners. A professor from Finland, who had nicknamed his bike "the Rolls Royce of Friendship Hotel," decided before departing to award it as a prize to the top student in one of his classes. But he was told the award would cause difficulties for the recipient. Colleagues and officials might raise questions about the propriety of such a gift. Some might regard it as a bribe. The Finn, just before he left, finally surrendered to the cultural difficulty and turned the bike over to me. I sold it for him to another foreign expert.

By the time Raija and I left China, our bikes had become extensions of us. We relied on them for business as well as for pleasure, and they had become prized possessions. We discussed shipping them home, but in the end, we did what nearly all long-term visitors do: we left the bikes behind, selling them for about the same price we had paid originally. Part of the "Chineseness" that remains with us today, though, comes from the joy we derived from our Phoenix and Flying Pigeon.

3 PEOPLE FLOWERS

Brightly colored lights resembling Christmas tree ornaments appeared one night on the front of the main building of the Friendship Hotel. Other buildings throughout Beijing sported similar decorations. In Tiananmen Square the lights were arranged to outline the shape of the structures. At about the same time, vendors popped up on the street corners selling fireworks. Flowers, whole gardens of flowers, sprang up overnight or during the day. Shops put up special displays emphasizing the variety and abundance of goods available. Above the toy section of the Number 1 department store on Wangfujing Street, a cardboard youngster, suspended from the ceiling, happily rode a giant fish, also made of cardboard. Meals in our dining hall and in restaurants became more elaborate.

It was late September, and a holiday mood was enveloping the city. On September 29, our Monday class meeting ended early. The Wednesday session was canceled. Some members of my class were going home for the first time since coming to Beijing in August.

The occasion was China's National Day—October 1, the anniversary of the 1949 founding of the People's Republic of China. It meant Christmas tree lights and Fourth of July fireworks, Thanksgiving feasts and Easter parades. It was Times Square and Red Square, Trafalgar and St. Peter's. It was an extravaganza that seemed to surprise everyone, the Chinese as well as us.

The fact that in 1986 China was celebrating the thirty-seventh anniversary of its founding was nothing extraordinary. What was special was the festive mood of the people. But more than that, it was the people. That's people as in "People's" Republic. Five million people, Raija and myself included, showed up in the heart of the nation's capital, Tiananmen Square. Five million! Crowd all of the people of

THRONGS OF CHINESE crowd into Tiananmen Square on China's National Day. In the background is the entrance to the Forbidden City, which the Chinese refer to as the Palace Museum.

Iowa and most of those in Kansas onto a one-hundred-acre farm, and you might approach five million. In China, you quickly become accustomed to seeing people everywhere, but not as many together in one place as on this National Day.

At one of my early class meetings, I had shown students slides of the University of Iowa campus and community. The photographs included downtown Iowa City (population about fifty thousand) during a summer noon hour. The photographs, of course, included people. Lots of them, I thought. Lunch crowds and shoppers. The students laughed. How could this place have "city" in its name? It was hardly a village. "More like . . ." began one student, who paused, stumped momentarily, and then with the help of others went on, "a ghost town." This was one of many adjustments we would have to make in our own conception of scale and size. The entire population of

Finland, when you think about it, would make up half the population of Beijing.

On this day, wherever you looked, wherever you walked — people. During the day and evening of September 30, more than three million people had visited the square, according to Beijing police chief Gao Ke. He was quoted in the *Beijing Daily* in an article under the banner headline "Beautiful Flowers, Good Hearts." Two million more flocked to the square the next two days.

"People mountains and people rivers," exclaimed one of my students.

Living in this city of about nine million for a little more than a month had not prepared us for National Day, one of four national holidays in China. The others are Spring Festival, which coincides with the Lunar New Year, the New Year according to the Western Gregorian calendar, and International Labor Day, May 1. While Spring Festival is a family celebration, National Day is a public and political event. This holiday was special for other reasons. It reflected the reforms implemented by the nation's leadership. The opening of doors to the world and an economic system restoring individual incentives have wrought a transformation in China. Though many deep personal scars remain, the Chinese people have begun to bounce back from the havoc of the Cultural Revolution and are participating in a massive effort to industrialize and modernize the nation.

My students affirmed the sense of optimism that prevailed in 1986. Of course, I do not consider my students typical; but to some extent they typified the emerging intellectuals in Chinese society. Most students said that, thanks to the leadership of Deng Xiaoping, they had been given an opportunity not only to take examinations and to qualify for more challenging positions but actually to make a career shift. Some went so far as to say that one day in their lives they might be able to hold and change jobs as they wish and not according to the dictate of the state.

The millions who thronged Tiananmen Square on National Day in 1986 offered the best evidence of the profound changes. Some say the square, the largest in the world, is a window and that the expressions of the people who flock there reflect the mood of China, as they wander among the towering monuments that tell the history of their country: Tiananmen Gate, the History Museum and the Museum of the Revolution, the Great Hall of the People, the Mao Zedong Mausoleum, and the Monument to the People's Heroes.

On this bright, warm, autumnal Wednesday, the square belonged to the people. Ordinary people making up an extraordinary throng dwarfed the monuments. Nearly lost in the tidal wave of humanity were the billboard-size portraits of Marx and Engels, side by side, and of Lenin and Stalin, also side by side, and the addition this year of Sun Yatsen. The presence of Sun Yatsen (1866–1925), who founded the Republic of China in 1912 and who is considered the father of his country, projected several messages. One was his three "People Principles"—nationalism, democracy, and livelihood. An underlying message was the goal of bringing together the "two Chinas," the mainland and Taiwan. As one of my students pointed out, the mainland at one time threatened unification by "capturing" Taiwan. The goal today is the same, but now China would like a peaceful merger under a policy of "one country, two systems," a slogan Chinese leaders have articulated in the planned takeover of Hong Kong. (Great Britain's lease on Hong Kong will expire in 1997, and China has pledged to maintain the island's social, economic, and political system.)

Opposite the portraits to the north, we could see the lone permanent portrait gracing the entrance to the Forbidden City (referred to by the Chinese as the Palace Museum), that of the Great Helmsman, Mao Zedong. Thirty-seven years ago to the day he had raised in the square the red, five-starred flag to found the new China.

Crowded into the square were Chinese from all over the country, including fourteen middle-aged women from the Ningxia Hui Autonomous Region who took the train to Beijing to observe National Day. They were typical of the holiday visitors who demonstrate—by their facial features and clothing—that China itself stands as a loosely unified country. More than fifty minority groups—from Tibet to Inner Mongolia, from Yunnan to Xinjiang—are represented in China. These minorities make up only 6.7 percent of the total population but occupy 50 to 60 percent of the land.

Trying to understand China's attitude toward minorities is a challenge. Our observations indicated that, for now at least, the country's leaders were showing special favor toward minority groups. On several occasions we visited the Minority Ethnic University (formerly the National Minorities Institute founded in 1951) not far from the Friendship Hotel. We also toured the Institute for Nationalities and the Yunnan Provincial Museum in Kunming. Despite well-intentioned efforts, ethnic tensions constantly surface, just as they do in the United States in Miami and other cities.

It is easy to criticize another nation's policy when it comes to civil rights, and such criticism is probably often deserved. But as China scholar John King Fairbank (1987, 103) points out, "before we beat the drum of human rights in our China policy, we need to sort out our global universals from culture-bound particulars and find common ground."

Diversity does not seem to trouble holiday crowds as they gather in the square among the multitudes of flowers. Days before the observance, the flowers had begun popping up all over the city, especially in Tiananmen Square. From wire and chrysanthemums a giant dragon sprang forth. Two oval water fountains appeared one day. Peacocks made of flowers settled in. Huge flower beds erupted into a riot of colors overnight. According to reports, one hundred thousand pots of flowers were brought to Tiananmen Square for the celebration. Still, the people made the day.

They were dressed as gaily as the flowers. The favorite pastime, apart from strolling, was taking pictures. Not just aiming and shooting, mind you, but carefully composing people and flowers, arranging, rearranging. Then a deep breath. Snap. Cherished memories of a good time getting better.

The sheer numbers of cameras underscored the prosperous times. An elderly Beijing resident, Jia Ren, said, "This time last year, the square was not as bright as now. I'm sure my photos will be a lot better than those I took last year." The decorations may have had something to do with his optimism. But so did the newly purchased Japanese camera hanging from his neck.

Often I assigned my students to write about certain events or topics. One such assignment was to write an article that dealt with the meaning of National Day. Ding Liguo, a graduate student from Hangzhou in tiny Zhejiang Province who has a degree from the Institute of International Relations, wrote: "This year [in Tiananmen Square] the political atmosphere is light. . . . Inspired by the open policy and economic reform, the Chinese people no longer take refuge in their historical glories. There has emerged a surge of reviewing Chinese cultural traditions in an attempt to explore elements which can be harmonized with the developing world."

As darkness fell on the square the night of October 1, a multitude of people turned toward the eastern sky to watch fireworks above the Workers' Stadium several miles away. Some three hundred thousand fans were there at a soccer game.

Once the party was over, the exodus from the square began. Motor traffic was at a standstill. It took an hour and a half to get a taxi. Many people walked home, and some gave up and stayed with friends whose lodgings were more accessible. Two days later, police chief Gao Ke reported there had been no accidents in Tiananmen Square during the celebration. No thefts either. As for the one hundred thousand pots of flowers, not one had been damaged or stolen.

Eight months later we participated in a national day celebration of another sort. Raija and I had been invited, along with hundreds of others, including Chinese, Americans, and other foreigners, to the U.S. Embassy to observe the Fourth of July. The affair was outdoors. A cardboard cutout of the Statue of Liberty stood atop one of the buildings in the compound, and beverages and hors d'oeuvres were served. A cutout of an eagle perched above the entrance to the residence of Ambassador Winston Lord and his wife, Betty Bao Lord, a writer of Chinese descent. Someone was dressed as Uncle Sam. A country western band was on hand. A trumpeter played "Stars and Stripes Forever" as Betty Bao Lord supervised the rolling out of a cart bearing a huge birthday cake. It was an extravaganza that kindled not so much the love of country, though that was part of the feeling, but more a sense of respect for heritage. Particular nationality, at that time and in that place, did not matter that much.

By afternoon Beijing had turned hot, and the Fourth of July festivities moved to several blocked-off streets in the Jianguomen Wai diplomatic area. Those who had purchased tickets were treated to McDonald's hamburgers and french fries that, we were told, had been brought from Hong Kong. There was a carnival and dancing. And you could buy T-shirts marking the occasion.

National day celebrations, wherever they are held, induce a sense of camaraderie and community. Maybe one day we will celebrate a truly international day.

4 REVEILLE AND
SHOE POLISH

One Saturday night, Raija and I, along with about fifty other foreign experts, found ourselves confined to the military base of Infantry Division No. 196 of the People's Liberation Army (PLA). We had arrived here peacefully after a two-hour bus ride east from Beijing. The weekend outing was to include Sunday in nearby Tianjin near the Yellow Sea.

None of us was certain what was in store for us at the military base. But we all felt a curiosity about China's army, the legendary feats of its soldiers during the country's long struggle, and, now, the impact of the nation's reforms. The visit was an unusual opportunity for visitors to learn about the Chinese army, and it also provided the military a chance to strut its stuff. Many of us had arrived in Beijing just a few weeks earlier and were a little apprehensive about spending a night at the base. Would we be able to leave according to schedule? What would we do there? Would we spend the night in barracks?

Our worries were unfounded. Greeting us warmly was vice-commander Zhu Fujin, a veteran of China's civil war against the nationalists (under Chiang Kaishek) and the war against Japan. He was more grandfatherly than military in his bearing. He and his lieutenants had been expecting our invasion and had prepared extensive maneuvers to impress and entertain us.

We arrived about 4 p.m. A hotly contested basketball game was taking place near headquarters, with standing spectators cheering on players who were stripped to their shorts. A larger-than-life statue of Mao Zedong marked base center. Red brick buildings and ponds dotted the flat countryside, which, we were told, had been rescued by this military unit from the desert and turned into farmland. Only a few uniformed soldiers were visible, including several stationed along the entrance route.

Commander Zhu directed us to the briefing room. We seated ourselves at long tables where tea was waiting. Flanked by officials of the foreign experts office who had arranged our trip, Commander Zhu recounted the history of Infantry Division No. 196. The unit, with about twelve thousand soldiers, including men and women, was established in 1937, having sprung up under Communist party chairman Mao Zedong. The division had fought more than two hundred battles, mostly in northern China. Because of their battlefield successes, two thousand soldiers from the division had been named "combat heroes." But Commander Zhu did not dwell on military accomplishments. He was more interested in telling us how this division had joined in the fight to develop the country economically. Things like pigs and shoe polish were on his mind.

"From the beginning," emphasized Commander Zhu, "our soldiers have been fighting and working side by side with ordinary people." It sounded almost like a quotation from Edgar Snow's *Red Star Over China*, a classic work originally published more than fifty years ago on China's struggle for unity and independence, and probably more popular in China than in the West. As an American journalist present at the turning point of modern Chinese history, Snow is among a handful of Westerners regarded as heroes by the Chinese. Near our hotel we had visited Snow's grave site, a small knoll at the end of a peaceful garden cove overlooking a lake on the Beijing University campus. (Half of Snow's ashes were placed in China at Snow's request, and the other half at Snedens Landing, New York.) Inscribed on the simple stone marker in English and Chinese is:

In Memory of Edgar Snow
American Friend of the Chinese People
1905–1972

In Snow's book, in a series of conversations recorded verbatim, Mao Zedong told how an early military force of the revolution had been referred to as the First Division of the First Peasants' and Workers' Army. Mao recognized early in his career that mobilization of the peasants was one—if not *the*—key to eventual military and political triumph. History, it turned out, was with Mao.

After the establishment of the People's Republic of China in 1949, many military units became permanent. They continue today to be identified with the populace. For example, the army provides educational training for the nation's youth as well as medical and other services for the public. The educational arm of the PLA provides several months of military training to university and college students. One aim is to prepare reserve soldiers and future officers.

Several of my students had served in the army. One had been a teacher in the Wuhan Radar School after studying Japanese as part of a military training team. Another, from Anhui Province, said he had enjoyed the military, adding, "If I had been born thirty years earlier, I would certainly go to war to fight against the Japanese." He hopes to cover military affairs as a journalist.

Commander Zhu was eager to show us around the base and to display proof that the people's army is also part of the nation's agricultural and industrial production effort.

First stop was the agricultural complex. Here the base annually raises more than eight hundred tons of grain, six hundred tons of vegetables, and livestock, including pigs. We stopped at several small factories, which produce, among other items, shoe polish and glue. One enterprise specializes in repairing clocks. The army barrack we also inspected resembled many facilities throughout China: spare, meager, austere. Yet we felt that most of the facilities, like my own classroom in Beijing, were functional and adequate. Such judgments, of course, are relative and involve expectations as well as what one is accustomed to. The wooden bunk beds held tightly drawn sheets and two folded blankets. A basin was underneath the bottom bunk.

All soldiers, including officers, are treated the same, we were told. They stay in the same quarters and use the same mess hall. In 1965 military ranks were abolished, and the PLA was held up as a model for citizens and communities to follow.

One of our stops on the base tour was the kitchen, where we were treated to fresh, sweet-tasting bread, warm soybean milk, and tofu. All these products had come from the base. This division, it would seem, could fight on its stomach.

Does the base produce a profit? Yes, said an officer. The money is used to support and modernize the base.

In China's economic reforms, the PLA, officially founded in 1927, has not fared so well. Although part of China's overall modernization program, the military's forces were sharply reduced and its budget cut. Further, it was told to keep pace with the rest of the nation's economy. One small indication of the new enterprise system is that in the past foreign experts were guests of the army. Not this year. We had to pay our way.

Actually, the fortunes of the military, like those of so many institutions in a period of rapid change, seem to fluctuate in relation to other social and political events. Following the antibourgeois campaign in 1987, the army gained a larger political voice in the power struggle between conservatives and reformists.

Another sign of the times is the push to promote PLA-made products at home and abroad. One company, Xinxing, has signed contracts worth $40 million U.S. with businesses in more than thirty countries. Products include everything from motorcycle engines to medicated toothpaste. A big seller in China has been a skin cream developed by army researchers to protect soldiers' skin. Now it is a popular beauty cream — Flying Rose Clouds brand 8403.

Up to this time, we really could not tell, except for the few military uniforms, that we were on a military base. Then we re-boarded the bus for a short drive to the firing range. From a mounted, glass-enclosed viewing stand, we watched deadly accurate sharpshooting. In one demonstration, ten crack shots scored ten hits at a distance of one hundred meters and then retrieved the targets to display them proudly to the visitors. Cannons also demolished targets nearly a mile away. A bazooka team did the same. The shots reverberating in the ears and the dust billowing in the distance made us thankful we were goodwill invaders.

The real he-man stuff was to come — a demonstration of martial arts and other physical feats. With a sledgehammer, one soldier broke a three-by-five-foot slab of stone six inches thick atop the chest of another soldier who was elevated, his head and feet resting on chairs. Bricks crumbled with the thrust of hands. Four bare-chested soldiers broke sixteen-ounce bottles against their heads. Afterward, with other guests, I went down to the performance area to verify that this was real glass and stone. It was.

After dinner back at headquarters, we toured the recreation center. We were told we could settle into the activity of our choice. The library was small but had quite a few newspapers and periodicals, nearly all in Chinese. In the music room we were treated to an officer's impromptu solo. He not only sang a song, but it was one of his own compositions. The Chinese have a penchant for amateur performances, and part of our group was cajoled into performing what may have been the Chinese premiere of the Hokey Pokey ("You put your right foot in . . . ").

Across the hall in another room, two civilian visitors parried shots across a Ping-Pong net. Meanwhile, upstairs the vice commander introduced us to the "electronic amusements room," in the words of the interpreter. The room featured variations on two computer Pac-Man games, pool, a form of chess called "go" (*weiqi* in Chinese), and, yes, Chinese checkers.

We spent the night in hotel-like accommodations at headquarters. Later we were told by a colleague that this is a model base often displayed to visitors. Indeed, subsequently we discovered that journalists are routinely taken to this base. The practice, one suspects, is universal, namely that most of us try to show off the best that we have to guests.

A footnote to the army visit came from my students. They were aware of my trip and were anxious to have me relate my experience. This was to be the case throughout the year. For who is not interested in how others perceive us? I was happy to share my observations with them. Near the end of my account of the visit, I mentioned, as a lighthearted afterthought, that the bed I had slept in at the base was very hard and that I was more than ready for an early morning reveille. No sooner had I spoken than several students began apologizing for the poor accommodations. They mistook my candor for complaint. It was not. Thereafter, I tried to weigh the cultural impact of my words before speaking.

5   RED BOOKS

A special feature of the Fulbright program in China is its funding for books. A professor can order multiple copies of certain titles and provide each student with his or her own copy. Dispensing these books becomes ceremonial. Students' eyes glisten. Fingers leaf gently through the pages. Are there any defects that would mar appearance? Ah, here's a word not encountered before. Hardbound books are coveted, but paperbacks are not rejected.

The book program is a recognition that books from the West are not readily available in China. The main reason is that books, as imported goods, must be paid for in foreign currency, which the Chinese do not have except through certain work units, overseas relatives, or the illegal black market. With the allotted book funds of $2,500, I had accumulated more than four hundred volumes. I had negotiated volume discounts from publishers and had begged books from my colleagues. About one-fourth of my library dealt with the history of the press and the role of mass media in society. The rest were primarily textbooks emphasizing techniques such as interviewing and writing. Also included were a few anthologies of outstanding journalistic writing.

After a tour of the modest library at the Journalism Institute, I decided to set up my own circulation system for students in my office. The institute library, though well stocked with Chinese periodicals, did not have contemporary works about the field of mass communication. The nearby, cramped library of the *China Daily* contained a much better collection of English-language works, including references, but access was limited. Moreover, the institute received only three American news magazines (*Time, Newsweek,* and *U.S. News &*

World Report), which were forwarded erratically to me and which I made available to students through my office.

My office was a spacious room a few steps from the classroom. It had a small refrigerator, in which colleagues stored lunch or fresh fruits; a table with a basin; the ubiquitous thermos of hot water, to which a coffee or tea sipper quickly develops an affinity; and two large desks with chairs. I shared the office with another teacher, Xiao Di, a young man who had an astounding facility with English and Chinese and taught translation. His English-born father, Michael Shapiro, had worked nearly forty years for the Xinhua news agency, and his Chinese mother had studied at the University of Minnesota and held a Ph.D. from Columbia. Early in the fall semester, Mr. Shapiro died at the age of seventy-six after a long illness, and Raija and I were among hundreds who attended a memorial service at the Babaoshan Revolutionary Cemetery.

Our office had no bookshelves. Searching out a certain book from eighteen boxes did not facilitate the learning enterprise. After several weeks, I was given a handsome six-by-four-foot bookcase with sliding glass doors to keep out the dust that permeates the city in the fall and spring. The case accommodated less than half of the book collection. A few weeks later, though, another bookcase arrived, and with two students serving as librarians, we set up the circulation system.

In the Fulbright book program, there is one stipulation: When teachers leave, they must leave the books behind. For a professor in China, few thrills approach being able to present books to Chinese students. Books are treasures. They are respected, used carefully, and displayed proudly. Not that books are expensive in China. In fact, books published in China are cheap, much cheaper than those in the United States. Raija and I purchased a number of English-language books published by the Foreign Language Press of China. Each cost about the same price ($1 to $2 U.S.) as an edition of the *International Herald Tribune* or the *South China Morning Post* from Hong Kong. Of course, one must take into account that while Chinese products are considerably cheaper than one is accustomed to, income in China is a fraction of income in the United States.

What made my books special is that most were not available anywhere else in China. That in itself was a sobering thought. You may have the only copy of a book among more than one billion people. It makes you want to take care of your books. Mine also were in English, and many were newly published.

At a Monday class meeting in mid-October, I told students that at the next session I would give each a copy of an anthology titled *The Best of Pulitzer Prize News Writing* (Publishing Horizons 1986). They would be able to read outstanding examples of journalism in the United States. At the same time they would improve their English and learn something about American culture.

The night before I planned to hand out the book, I decided to browse through it once again. Suddenly one of the entries I had not paid much attention to caught my eye. It carried the dateline "Yonpo Airstrip, Korea." The 1951 Pulitzer Prize–winning article was by veteran war correspondent Keyes Beech of the now-defunct *Chicago Daily News*. In this new setting, I decided to read the piece again. The article graphically told of the fighting withdrawal in December 1950 of the United States First Marine Division from the Changjin Reservoir. The story reported that thousands of Chinese troops had been engaged, perhaps as many six divisions totaling sixty thousand men.

Halfway through the story, I leaped out of my chair.

"One company killed so many Chinese," read the report, "the Marines used their frozen bodies as a parapet. But for every Chinese they killed there were five, ten or twenty to take his place."

There was more.

" 'What'n hell's the use in killing them,' said one Marine. 'They breed faster'n we can knock 'em off.' "

This did not seem to bode well for classroom rapport. I began having second thoughts. I had inscribed in the twenty-one copies the name of each student and the date. The reason for this was to try to make sure that the books would stay in the hands of the students rather than being claimed by the work unit as the collective owner. Just before class, I decided to substitute another book.

Months passed. I fretted over how I could dispose of these books in a suitable way. A book burning would be sacrilegious. In China it would be reminiscent of the Cultural Revolution, when many books and libraries were destroyed. What a problem! How to get rid of books in a nation short of books, a nation that had invented printing as early as the Tang dynasty (618–907) and had, at least until the eighteenth century, printed more books than all the rest of the world combined.

I finally hit upon a plan. I would give the books to the students, together with a lecture on the importance of historical context. I rehearsed the brief speech. For now I not only had to try to explain the ethnic slur and the Korean War but also the old date I had inscribed in each copy of the book. This was becoming even more difficult than the extemporaneous lecture I had been asked to give one afternoon on the theory and practice of baseball. Try to explain "home run" or the reputation of Babe Ruth and the relationship of the two to someone who has never heard of either. It was World Series time, and my remarks were an orientation to a movie the students were to see, *The Natural*. Luckily for everyone, there was not a quiz afterward.

In the problem of distributing the Pulitzer collection, there was one small point in my favor: the book had a bright red cover. It was the little red book of Pulitzer—not Mao—reporting. The whole world, of course, is familiar with "the little red book" titled *Quotations of Chairman Mao*. The Mao book was studied and memorized by the Chinese during the mid and late 1960s in an attempt by leaders to restore the nation's revolutionary spirit. Photographs that came to be a cliché in the Western media showed Chinese youth shouting and waving copies of the book. My students were not that excited about this new red book, but they were eager nonetheless.

After the standard fifteen-minute class break, I asked several students to help me carry the books from my office into the classroom.

"Many things change over the years," I intoned. "Only a few years ago I could not even have come to this classroom."

The class stirred. They were impatient. The books were on their minds, and they wanted them in their hands.

"Now I'm going to give you a copy of a book which contains several passages that may offend you. Believe me, I do not want to offend you. In fact, I thought of not giving you this book at all. Maybe destroying them."

Several class members winced.

"Even though none of you had probably been born yet, the Korean War of the early 1950s saw American and Chinese soldiers fighting each other. There was a lot of bloodshed. And it was not a good time for American and Chinese relations."

Students, puzzled over what was going on, began fidgeting.

"Our journalists covered that war," I pressed on, "and some of the reporting was considered exceptional."

I held up a copy of the book.

"In this book a reporter writes about American and Chinese soldiers fighting and killing each other.

"I wanted you to know that I regret that this article appears in this book. Nonetheless, I think there are some excellent examples of outstanding reporting in this book. And that's why I want to present it to you."

I had more to say, but by now students sensed what was going on. Zeng Lintong, sitting at the end of the second row next to the window, ever alert and always willing to help, was waiting for a pause in my comments. When it came, he said, "We understand that times change and that our countries have not always been friendly. But none of us here is responsible for what happened."

His classmates nodded. And another added, "So, can we have the books now?"

I shut up and gave out the books. The students devoured this new red book. They not only admired the superb examples of Western news writing but also wound up dividing themselves into teams and translating the entire collection into Chinese.

The lesson for the day was clear: Not only do red books change, but so do times.

6 COBWEBS
AND EMPERORS

History can be learned in a variety of
ways, including from children. An
example occurred the day in November 1986 when Raija and I visited the
Forbidden City. A boy six or seven years old, wearing a white shirt, a
light red bandanna around his neck, and what looked like a Cub
Scout cap, ran toward an old man in a dirty, rumpled gray shirt who
was shuffling up stairs toward the throne from which emperors had
ruled China.

As the old man, cap in left hand, stepped over a restraining rope,
the youngster shouted, "Stop. You are not allowed in there."

"Who are you?" inquired the old man.

"I live here. I'm the son of the guardian."

"Uh, well," responded the old man. "I used to live here too." He
pointed his right arm toward the throne. "That is where I sat."

There? In the Hall of Supreme Harmony? In the Imperial Palace
of China?

"Who are you?" repeated the puzzled youngster.

"I was the emperor of China."

"Prove it."

The old man, wan and bespectacled, continued up the stairs and
then stopped, seated himself on the throne, leaned back, and with his
left arm withdrew a small, round container. He wiped off the dust and
cobwebs with his cap and held it out to the youngster.

The boy and the old man did this once. Twice. Three times. Four.
And more. I lost count. Where were all those cobwebs coming from?

Surely the Italian film crew, which had brought truckloads of
pasta and cheese and mineral water from Italy, could not have an

THERMOS IN HAND, John Lone takes a break from shooting a final scene of *The Last Emperor* in the Temple of Supreme Harmony in the Forbidden City.

army of spiders tucked away busily spinning webs just for this scene. But who really knew? Moviemaking can be as unreal as the movies that are made.

The cobwebs came from an electrical device resembling a large eggbeater. The webs were mass-produced. The man working the machine was prepared for as many "takes" as necessary. Spiders need not have applied.

This fast-web service was part of the filming of a $23-million movie that was made in China under famed Italian director Bernardo Bertolucci (*The Last Tango in Paris, 1900, The Conformist*). The title of this film: *The Last Emperor.*

Raija and I had Imperial courtside seats at this day's shooting. We were to play tourists in one of the closing scenes. It was our—if you'll permit stretching the phrase to the breaking point—acting debut. At the time we did not know it, but we were entering a door of Chinese history marked by chaos and confusion. You might have heard of some of the other cast members—Peter O'Toole, John Lone (star of *Year of the Dragon*), and Joan Chen. But first we must go to the beginning of this saga, in which we were catapulted backward into Chinese history and forward onto the silver screen.

The night before the filming, a couple also living in the Friendship Hotel had stopped by to ask if we would like to serve as extras in a closing scene of a movie. As foreign experts spending a year in China as editors at the magazine *China Reconstructs,* they had been asked to recruit potential extras. They did not know much about the movie, but they obviously had a keen eye for acting talent. They were from California, and that's somewhere near Hollywood.

Raija and I, along with about a dozen other Westerners who auditioned on the basis of being at the right place at the right time, were to report at the East Gate of the Forbidden City at 9:30 a.m. the next day. We were not about to hold up this multimillion-dollar production, to which Bertolucci already had devoted two years of negotiating with the Chinese. We were there by 9:00.

A young woman, Ulrike, was in charge of casting. She was dressed in close-fitting corduroys, spoke with a German accent, and was wearing sunglasses. Already we were acting like amateurs—we had forgotten our sunglasses. But Ulrike knew her business, and she approved us at a glance. It was our first screen test.

Nearby were power generators, truckloads of film equipment, and dozens of production crew members—all brought from Italy or Great Britain. The language on the set was polyglot; the film was to be in English.

Ulrike directed us to a van, which took us to the Hall of Supreme Harmony, our shooting location for this early November day. She gave us our first instruction: "Wait."

From a distance we could see arrangements being made for the day's work. There were people tending to lighting, sound, makeup. Several men were hammering boards together. Others were prying boards apart. And there was a workman not resembling a spider at all who was fiddling with the eggbeater.

Although novices, we could follow instructions. We waited.

10:00.

11:00. Ulrike came by, extended her palms down, and moved her hands up and down. We understood. By now rumor had it that we were going to be paid for this. Professionals can handle waiting.

Noon. As far as I could tell, the crew had not done any filming yet. With the kind of budget we were operating on, obviously we were settling for nothing less than perfection. An Oscar could be at stake.

The Hall of Supreme Harmony is the heart of the Forbidden City, so named because it was off-limits to ordinary folks for five centuries. The Hall is the tallest and largest of the nearly one thousand Palace Museum buildings in the Forbidden City. It had limited use: ceremonies such as the emperor's birthday, the nomination of military leaders, and coronations. Inside is the richly decorated Dragon Throne, where emperors presided.

Our movie was the first time that a film crew had been permitted to shoot in the Forbidden City. So what's a little waiting?

An estimated ten thousand people visit the Forbidden City every day. Ironically, during our shooting, certain buildings were forbidden to visitors. In feudal times violators would have been executed.

1:00 p.m. I worked myself to an observation point just outside the hall. A hush fell over the set. They had begun shooting a scene. Not ours. Ulrike came by; she nodded knowingly, we nodded understandingly.

Nearly 2:00 p.m. Ulrike came rushing over. "Time to eat," she said. We were ready. It had been tiring. Making movies is not easy.

We piled into a van, drove to a nearby building within the Forbidden City, and sat down to an Italian meal of minestrone, pasta, chicken and potatoes, cheese, and mineral water. The Italians, we discovered later, had brought forty-four hundred pounds of pasta and Parmesan cheese and nearly fifty thousand pounds of Italian bottled mineral water. Food could not be blamed if we did not produce a good movie. The production crew joined us, but Bernardo was probably busy elsewhere.

3:00 p.m. We were back on the set. They were shooting the scene with the boy and the old man. The man with the eggbeater was as busy as, well, a spider.

The film is about Pu Yi (also known as Henry Pu Yi). He is — or was — China's last emperor. On the death in 1908 of the tyrant, Empress Dowager Wu Cixi (Tzu Hsi), Pu Yi ascended to the throne. He was two years old. The Hall of Supreme Harmony was Pu Yi's romper room; the throne, his playpen. Little did Pu Yi know it would be downhill from then on.

At the age of six, he was removed from the throne when the Republic of China was proclaimed on January 1, 1912. Dr. Sun Yatsen became provisional president of the unsteady new republic and shortly afterward gave up the post to Yuan Shikai. Foreign incursions and internal administrative strife followed. The very existence of the republic was threatened.

Meanwhile, amid opulence and thousands of eunuchs, Pu Yi was growing up in the Forbidden City. Finally, in 1924, he was expelled by the Chinese warlords who took control of the government.

Pu Yi took refuge with the Japanese in Tianjin, and following Japan's invasion of Manchuria in northeast China, he was installed as puppet emperor of the land the Japanese referred to as Manchukuo (country of the Manchu). He remained as a figurehead until 1945, when he was taken prisoner by the Soviet Union. Shortly after 1949, the Soviets returned Pu Yi to China. Everyone expected Pu Yi to be executed. Instead he was imprisoned for reeducation. His education apparently was complete by 1959, when Mao Zedong freed him. Pu Yi was given a job as a gardener in the Botanical Garden in Beijing. He died in 1967.

Now, on an autumnal day, the sun was warming the marble terrace and visitors were being directed around the massive courtyard in front of the Temple of Supreme Harmony. An elderly Pu Yi, played by John Lone, was returning to the scene of his early childhood, when he was literally China's last emperor. At this point Peter O'Toole had already finished his work on the film. He portrayed the Scot, Sir Reginald Johnston, tutor to the young emperor.

Finally the last spider web had been spun, and the scene was, as we say, "in the can." It was approaching 4:30. The day's shooting had been exhausting, and we had not even begun our scene yet. But we were pros — or we would be as soon as we were paid.

We were told to go into the hall. Our instructions were to stand at the entranceway and, when given the word, to walk toward the throne like tourists. We had been pondering the part since early morning. We had it down pat.

Constantine, one of Bernardo's assistants, checked the lighting.

ON LOCATION inside the Temple of Supreme Harmony in China's Forbidden
City, Bernardo Bertolucci (left) consults
with assistants about shooting a scene for
The Last Emperor.

Another assistant, megaphone in hand, gave us instructions. "Get
ready," he told us in English. "Ack-shione," he said in Italian-English.
We all marched forward. "Try it again," we were told. We did it again.
And again.

Bertolucci himself was directing the scene. It was becoming clear
that it took a lot to satisfy him. Wearing a brown cap, green jacket

with plaid scarf, and brown pants, he stalked the set with grace. An eyepiece hung from his neck.

After six takes, we almost got it right. Then there was a pause. Pu Yi, alias John Lone, dressed in that rumpled gray Mao suit, entered the scene. He was placed among a group of Chinese tourists, who, as with us Westerners, were to be touring the hall. The last emperor—who had gone from riches to rags—was now a tourist in what was once his palace. A nice touch, I thought. It was good to be working for Bertolucci.

Two more takes. On the eighth one we got it right. It was an exhilarating feeling. Even Bertolucci seemed pleased. Raija, my co-star, talked to him and got his autograph. But soon he returned to business, moving toward the throne, sizing it up for the next shooting.

Ulrike motioned us to follow her. She asked us to wait. By now, we had mastered this part. Before long Ulrike gave each of us a small, greenish pay envelope sporting in small type the note that it had been manufactured in Kalamazoo, Michigan. Inside were three crisp $10 U.S. notes.

Professionals that we now were, we decided it was time to celebrate. "Pizza," someone suggested. It seemed appropriate. Pizza was not easy to find even in this city of nine million, but we found it at the Jianguo Hotel.

The movie opened in the United States in late 1987, months after we had left China. The early reviews were not favorable. Vincent Canby of the *New York Times* (November 20, 1987) called the movie "an elegant travel brochure . . . a let-down . . . [the film] works most effectively as an illustrated introduction to modern Chinese history." So what's wrong with that? we mused. It was not long before the Academy of Motion Pictures and Sciences announced its nominations. *The Last Emperor* was nominated for nine awards and won in all nine categories. One of the Oscars was for best director and another for best film.

After the announcement of the awards, Richard Bernstein, a former China correspondent, also writing in the *New York Times* (May 8, 1988), criticized the accuracy of the film. He wrote that the movie, "for all of its authenticity of detail, may be less diligent as history: It seems to accept . . . the official Chinese Communist version of the facts."

Perhaps we had become biased participants, but in our estimation Bertolucci produced a remarkable film dealing with a history that, by and large, Americans are not familiar with. And perhaps it is useful once in a while to question our own version of events.

Final scene. Last take. Do we actually show up in the film? Yes. We first saw the movie thirteen months after we had left China. It was opulent and sweeping, an epic. It was also engrossing and generally accurate. If we had not been familiar with some of the historical events, I do not think we would have been able to follow the story. The film provided a unique remembrance of a memorable time.

As we left the theater, any illusions of grandeur disappeared. Not one person in the audience recognized in their midst the two members of the cast who just moments earlier had loomed larger than life on the screen. Had everyone blinked at the same time during our instant of stardom?

7 SCOOP

On a warm November afternoon, more than four hundred persons crowded into the auditorium of the main building of the Friendship Hotel. Extra chairs were set up, but there were not enough. People did not mind standing. The event was a forum arranged by the State Bureau of Foreign Experts for foreign experts in Beijing, most of whom worked as teachers or editors for educational and cultural institutions. They obviously were interested in the topic of the forum: a discussion of Chinese literature by a group of thirteen Chinese writers. The forum included a speech by Wang Meng, minister of culture and a noted author himself.

Probably no topic stirs deeper feelings inside and outside China than that of freedom of expression. Are writers free to write whatever they want? How far can they go in dealing with sensitive topics, such as religion or sex? How critical can they be of the political leadership? The trend in China in the past decade had been toward greater freedom of expression and more openness. This expanding freedom emerged as the dominant theme of the discussion. But as would be demonstrated only a few weeks after the forum, brakes can be applied abruptly. When this happens, results produce anxiety and confusion. How far can we go now? How long will it take for things to blow over this time? It is a cliché to describe change in China as one step forward and half a step backward.

When I told my students on that Wednesday morning about the meeting of writers, they were excited. All wanted to attend, and it seemed an excellent reporting assignment for the class. They were beginning to exhibit some of the journalistic traits that we occasionally talked about in class. This involved taking initiative, developing a sense for news, overcoming their shyness in conducting interviews, and, in general, developing self-confidence.

When we dealt with such matters, I was always slightly self-conscious. What kind of influence was I having on the students and their outlook on journalism? Would it make problems for them later in their careers? Was I evaluating their performance strictly by Western standards? How could I be sensitive to their cultural, including political, environment? I wrestled with these questions often. I usually concluded that as a teacher I could teach only what I know. The teacher should introduce — not impose — practices and ideas. The teacher's obligation is to help students develop intellectual and artistic talents to the fullest. Of course, this philosophy itself derives from my own cultural upbringing. Though I was critical of the way journalism was practiced in China, I constantly tried to place my views in a larger historical and cultural framework. After all, I had been invited to come here, presumably to teach what I knew.

Thus, in a way, I was pleased at the students' interest in attending the literature forum. But it did not seem feasible for everyone to attend. The session had been planned ostensibly for foreign experts, and seating would be limited.

"I don't know if any reporter will be covering this," I told the students. "But I would think this would be a newsworthy event."

During class break, one student, Wang Xiangwei, dashed to the editorial offices of the *China Daily* and asked if the newspaper planned to staff the event. At twenty-one, Wang Xiangwei was among the youngest and most gifted students in the class, and he was also the tallest, matching my height of six feet, two inches. He was from the city of Jilin in the northern province of Jilin, which borders North Korea. Among this group of students, who knew English well, he was probably the best. Before enrolling in the journalism program, he had graduated from the Foreign Languages Institute in Beijing, where he also had come under the influence of an American journalism professor. After a brief consultation, Wang Xiangwei heard the first part of the response he wanted. No, no plans had been made to cover the meeting, an editor told him. Could I cover it? he asked. He got the second part of his response: Go ahead. It was to be his first big "scoop" in a land where scoops are not common.

Since a taxi could accommodate a total of four passengers, two other students accompanied Wang Xiangwei and me to the hotel after lunch. We were forty-five minutes early, but already people were streaming into the second-floor meeting room.

Delayed by attempts to find additional seating, the program began with cultural minister Wang Meng sketching the recent history of Chinese literature. He said writers were one of the groups benefiting most from Deng Xiaoping's reform policies.

"As compared to the past, writers now have a more stable life and have greater freedom of creativity," he said. "Between 1977 and 1980 there was a great craze for literature. Readers were looking for new, daring ideas in literature—and also for political insights. In the '80s everything was written about."

The past two years, he said, had seen new emphasis on freedom of creativity. "It is hard to say what the prevailing viewpoint is on literature in China today. No one idea or thing is prevalent today."

When he brought up the topic of censorship, a hush fell upon the crowd. He had complete attention.

Contrary to some views, he said, not all Chinese works of literature and art had to undergo government censorship. "Technically it is not feasible to read all the output of short stories, novels, and so on. Every year China produces ten thousand short stories, one thousand medium-length stories, and over one hundred novels. If the government had to censor all of these, the State Council [China's highest administrative body] would have to become a 'reading club.' "

His open acknowledgment of the existence of censorship surprised everyone. It also emphasized the unusual openness that, for the time being at least, reflected the climate of expression in China.

"Some books on some subjects have to be examined before being published," he went on. The subjects included religion, minority groups, and persons in sensitive positions. He did not elaborate on those topics. (Religious worship, once prohibited, has returned. Though we visited many temples and churches, indications were that religious interest was no more than modest and often merely attracted the curious. As for minorities, China has had to contend with more than fifty different groups, many of whom, such as the Tibetans, adhere to their own practices and customs. The reference to people in sensitive positions apparently referred to political leaders.)

Wang Meng discussed the relationship between the Communist party leadership and artistic freedom. "Party leadership has to carry out policies. Thus, literary creation, in this sense, is under the party. The same can be said about the production of beer and food. The party does not have a direct hand in the control. The party is also interested in creating more favorable conditions for writers to be able to work.

"In writing, there is only one god—the god of yourself. Writers can be more fruitful in a more democratic, modern environment. The Communist party and common people have a common stake in building a modern, democratic environment."

Someone asked Wang Meng why the Chinese were concerned about the Nobel Prize. His answer was short, "Because no Chinese has ever won it." The response begged the question.

It is true that no Chinese writer has ever won the Nobel Prize for Literature. This lack of recognition has become a point of irritation for Chinese writers and an embarrassment for the intellectual community. A Chinese delegation had even visited the Royal Swedish Academy to explore the issue. The question posed is a nagging one. Has the Nobel Prize eluded Chinese writers because of political constraints that hamper Chinese writers? Indeed, the climate of creative expression tends to be cyclical, wavering in relation to the political winds of the moment. Or is it the language? Translations of Chinese ideographs are difficult to accomplish at best, and no matter how faithful, they tend to lose something of the original.

Taking the spotlight at the meeting was Zhang Xianliang, a youthful (fifty), energetic, outspoken, and controversial writer who has challenged the establishment—and readers—by probing topics considered taboo, such as sex. His works have won awards and been turned into movies. They include *Mimosa* (1984) and *Half of Man Is Woman* (1985). The latter novel, translated by Martha Avery and published in the United States in 1988, uses sex—more particularly, impotence—as a metaphorical indictment of the decade-long trauma the Cultural Revolution brought to China. Zhang has spent twenty years in prison and at hard labor in China's gulag.

He told the audience he had not expected the uproar that followed the publication of his novels, which, he said, deal with very natural subjects. He said his years in prison were liberating. He put it this way: "When a person loses his physical freedom, the mind becomes completely free.

"The novels I have written purely express my ideas and thoughts," Zhang said. "In my novels I presented what I have heard, seen, and felt."

As the audience and writers divided into small groups for discussion, my student Wang Xiangwei, now an intrepid journalist, rushed for a telephone to consult his editors. He summarized for them what had happened and what had been said. They were incredulous at the cultural minister's remarks about censorship, that he would even broach the topic so openly and candidly. What proof of such remarks

AUTHOR ZHANG XIANLIANG signs autographs following a forum on Chinese literature at the Friendship Hotel in Beijing.

did student Wang have? He said he could probably get an audio tape of the discussion. They told him to get it.

Wang Xiangwei knew that I had made a cassette tape recording of the discussion.

"Can I borrow your tape?" he asked.

"Of course."

By now it was 5:30 p.m. He had to make his way back to the

newsroom by public bus. With the deadline approaching (the *China Daily* is a morning newspaper), he hurriedly wrote the story.

The editors approved. And there, on Thanksgiving Day, November 27, 1986, emblazoned in five columns across the bottom of page 1, was the headline: "Foreigners get to quiz Chinese writers." The byline, which could not convey the persistence and resourcefulness of the evolution of the story, simply read: "by Wang Xiangwei."

In all likelihood, the forum would not have taken place at all had it been scheduled a month or two later. And if it had taken place, it is unlikely a report of it would have appeared on page 1 of the *China Daily.* For the moment, though, the intellectual climate was warm and pleasant.

In a few days December would arrive. Raija and I would be on our way to Shanghai for two weeks of lectures at Fudan University. Colder weather and student demonstrations were coming.

II

二

8 STUDENT PENDULUM

On the Saturday morning of December 20, 1986, I left Fudan University's guest house to walk to the campus a block away. Some landmarks were familiar to me from my visit two years before. The small shops and bustling activity continued along narrow Guonian Road. Just beyond the brick columns and swinging steel gates at the entrance of the university was the larger-than-life statue of Mao Zedong, standing majestically in topcoat with chest out, hatless, hands behind the back.

Fudan, founded in 1905 and one of China's premier universities, sprawls over thirty square acres in the northeast suburbs of Shanghai. The campus is a lush garden. In the early morning, students stroll the campus reciting lessons. With six to eight students to a room, there is little privacy. Tree-lined walkways provide a natural study habitat. Though Shanghai lies in a temperate zone, a chill penetrates the air in December and a light coat is necessary. In the unheated classrooms, students sit in padded garments. Some take notes with gloves, the tips cut off to facilitate writing.

Some things, I noticed, had changed. The campus had spilled beyond its compound. A new, modern library now stands across from the entranceway, and nearby a high-rise building occupies a recreation field where one early morning I had jogged to the blast of marching music played over loudspeakers. The structure houses Fudan's liberal arts program.

Approaching the entrance gate, I noticed students crowded around a bulletin board reading posters written by hand. Bicycles had been parked temporarily in the drive. The writing was in Chinese. I wanted to be on time for my guest lecture to a journalism class, so I pressed on. A few minutes later, I was inside the classroom, where I was to continue a series of lectures to students planning to become

59

AT FUDAN UNIVERSITY in Shanghai, students gather around a bulletin board to read announcements about the massive demonstrations that occurred the night before.

journalists. The topic for the day, appropriately, was news flow in the world. Before I could even begin speaking, though, students were questioning me. The topic was news flow of a different sort:

"Do you know what's going on?"

"What do you think of the demonstrations?"

"Shouldn't our press be covering this story?"

This was my introduction to what were at that point the largest peaceful demonstrations in China in ten years. As in many other nations, young people were the vanguard of the protest for change. Some twenty years earlier in the United States, I had experienced similar feelings. At that time, many American universities, fearing violence such as that at Kent State, had ended the spring semester early and told students to leave the campus.

In China, student protests have played an important role histori-cally in social and political change. Students are part of a tiny intellectual elite. Perhaps the most famous protest occurred May 4, 1919, when students triggered a widespread reformist movement protesting a decision of the Paris Peace Conference to award German properties in China to Japan. The whole nation responded. The result was a movement to modernize China, with democracy and science as major themes. The spark setting off the movement — referred to as the May Fourth Movement — was a demonstration by three thousand students from Beijing universities and educational institutions at Tiananmen Gate, the entrance to the Forbidden City. The protests led indirectly to the founding of the Communist party in 1921.

Now, suddenly, here I was in China in the midst of a major student outburst. What did the discontent mean? What was at issue? What did this mean in terms of changes now taking place in China? What would be the long-term impact? I tried to sort through these and other questions.

What emerged was a tight web of interrelated events that may defy the Western mind and certainly underscores cultural differences. "Inscrutable" is the usual way we explain the inexplicable when it happens in China. But that seems to be an excuse when reason fails or intolerance prevails.

A few weeks later, after Raija and I had returned to Beijing, I continued searching for meaning amidst the turbulence, which by now had been blared worldwide by non-Chinese news media. First, there was the problem of simply finding out what was going on. The midst of a commotion is not necessarily the best vantage point. Second, there was the difficulty of identifying the reasons for student discontent. When not cloaked in generalities, the reasons varied from campus to campus. Third, there was the enormous challenge of trying to put these events into the context of contemporary developments in China, especially the much-heralded reform movement and open-door policy. This was the hardest thing to do.

When students in Shanghai asked me what I knew about the demonstrations, I discovered I knew more than they did. Thanks to a shortwave radio, I had listened that morning to the VOA (Voice of America) and the BBC (British Broadcasting Corporation), the two best sources for keeping abreast of breaking news in China. The Chinese are avid listeners too, with as many as twenty million listening at least once a week to the VOA.

The Shanghai students had not even heard about the protests a few days earlier at Shenzhen University, just across from Hong Kong in a zone marked by China for special economic development.

Shenzhen students were reported to have overturned cars and thrown rocks. The Shanghai demonstrations, easily the largest in China, began December 19, 1986, and spread to at least a dozen cities before abating.

My main source for information about campus disturbances in China was the *South China Morning Post* published in Hong Kong. This British-style newspaper, which came under Rupert Murdoch's primary ownership in November 1986, is still the best and most complete daily source of what is going on in China today. At that time, you could not always get it at the Beijing newsstands. When something newsworthy, at least by Western journalistic standards, was happening in China, copies got snapped up quickly. As far as I know, no issues of this newspaper or any other foreign papers (including *USA Today,* the *International Herald Tribune,* and the *Times of London*) and newsmagazines were denied entry to China during this time. A smattering of headlines from issues of the *South China Morning Post* encapsulated the story of the demonstrations:

> *December 18:* "Shenzhen student violence overturns higher fees plan" (on page 1).
> *December 24:* "Marching students defy Shanghai police orders" (on page 1).
> *December 28:* "China's Restless Youth" (special Sunday "Spectrum" report).
> *December 30:* "Students defy authorities in illegal march."

At the end of 1986, the story moved to Beijing. In the area around the Friendship Hotel, where we lived, are many of the city's universities and educational institutions, including the Beijing, Qinghua, and People's universities. In the cold December air, late at night, students marched past the hotel along Baishiqiao Road.

> *January 4:* "Exam pressure could delay China protests."

Indeed, the fall semester was coming to an end. A month-long holiday in observance of the Chinese New Year was about to begin. Some institutions disbanded classes early.

> *January 12:* "Deng [Xiaoping] orders party crackdown on liberals" (on page 1).

The pendulum swung with the sharpest-yet response from the Communist party. Chinese leader Deng Xiaoping was quoted as saying, "We can afford to shed some blood. Just try as much as possible not to kill anyone."

The next day's page 1 headline was foreboding: "The backlash begins . . ."

Someone has described the news about China that comes into China through foreign media as "exported imports." Since I paid attention to foreign media, I was better informed about some things in China than most Chinese. The media created two different perceptions of China, neither one of which I felt comfortable with. The foreign media stories bordered on sensationalism and lacked context. The Chinese media ignored events considered unpleasant or simply glossed over them.

Another good source of information about events that went unreported in the Chinese media was the Friendship Hotel's Dining Hall No. 8. Here is where several hundred foreign experts congregated daily to eat and exchange information. The trouble with this was that no one had sifted hearsay from actual events. Rumors were rampant.

The Chinese media finally could no longer ignore the student protests, which apparently were having greater repercussions than anticipated. The coverage was late and obviously orchestrated. The outburst of campus demonstrations appeared to have begun the first week in December in Anhui and Hubei provinces. The Chinese media broke their silence on December 20 when a report quoted a State Education Commission official as saying that the demonstrations were legal and would not be suppressed as long as they were not against the law.

Coverage increased. But the tone quickly shifted to reports of student demonstrators' disrupting traffic and interfering with citizens' day-to-day activities. A few troublemakers were to blame, officials were quoted as saying. There was also enough blame for Taiwan, which was accused of helping to foment student unrest for its own political purposes, and the VOA, which was charged with encouraging the demonstrators. The nation's official Communist party voice, the *People's Daily,* urged restraint and attacked those deviating from the party's four cardinal principles — socialism, Marx-Lenin-Mao Zedong thought, leadership of the party, and dictatorship of the proletariat. They were, the paper claimed, promoting "bourgeois liberalization," an epithet equated with capitalism. The *China Daily,* the English-language newspaper read avidly by visitors to China, took its editorial cue from the *People's Daily* and Xinhua, the nation's official news agency.

Students at nearby Beijing University were upset by what they felt was distorted coverage by the Chinese media of the demonstrations. They publicly burned copies of the *Beijing Daily,* a state-run newspaper published by city authorities.

One of the few media in China to score journalistically from the demonstrations was China Central Television (CCTV). On the evening of December 30, CCTV dramatically launched its new English news service with an extensive report of the demonstrations. The program emphasized the government point of view and featured a report of an interview given by He Dongchang, vice-minister of the State Education Commission. Pictures from the Shanghai demonstrations accompanied the report.

Throughout the demonstrations, Western journalists had a heyday. Here was a story they could see and experience without contending with bureaucratic obstacles. Perspective was a frequent casualty.

As to what was behind the protests, students were asking for freedom, democracy, and human rights. These demands translated into many things. In Shenzhen, students were objecting to a university proposal tying tuition costs to classroom performance: students with high grades would pay less tuition than students with poor grades. The idea died aborning.

In Shanghai, students I talked to were concerned with lack of press freedom, the low salary structure after graduation, and the little, if any, job choice. Elsewhere, students complained they could not elect representatives to governing bodies, and some objected to the low quality of food. One student told me, "The media don't even carry news of our demonstrations." I asked about the campus newspaper. There was, I was told, one newspaper, *Youth Union,* published under the auspices of Communist party officials.

But students did have the handwritten posters that over the centuries have figured prominently in communicating information in China. Frustrated and impatient at the agonizingly slow pace of the reforms, students used the posters to reflect the depth of their discontent. Messages were bold and sarcastic and displayed the authors' courage or foolhardiness, depending on your point of view. Here are some of the messages displayed at Beijing University, as reported in the *Far Eastern Economic Review,* a weekly newsmagazine published in Hong Kong:

> The [Communist] party is not a completely perfect organization and particularly at present has many shortcomings. . . . Does

> maintaining the leadership of the party mean that we must always do everything the party says? Does it mean that we cannot criticize the party?

> In the U.S. there is the false freedom to support or not support the communist party. In our country, we have the genuine freedom of having to support the communist party. In the U.S. there is the false freedom of the press, but in our country we have the genuine freedom of no freedom of the press.

> We write the big character posters because it is the only way we can express our opinions. There is no crime in the posters, but now some people want to close off our only breathing hole, letting us quietly suffocate under layers of mud and dirt, and thereby regain social stability and unity. A big character poster is a tool of speech and expression, and its function is completely determined by the objective of its writer, not the nature of the medium itself.

In Beijing, my students — many old enough to have experienced the nightmare of the Cultural Revolution — echoed the complaints. But they cautioned against moving too quickly. They said action must be accompanied by a sense of social responsibility. Further, they had had instructions from officials not to get involved, even as bystanders.

One of my students may have inadvertently put his finger on another key issue that had not drawn much attention. In a major reporting assignment for my class, he described student dissatisfaction in the classroom. Students he interviewed complained that required courses in Marxist philosophy, political economics, scientific socialism, and the history of the Chinese Communist party were of little practical use. Furthermore, they grumbled about being taught by dull and uninterested professors.

Said one professor: "There's no denying that basic courses on Marxist tenets are being challenged. The long-standing difficulty in our teaching has really embarrassed us." Students reacted as students anywhere would. They wrote letters in class, read magazines, dozed off, or simply did not show up.

The article written for my class was by a talented student. His work was good enough to appear regularly in Chinese publications, but this particular story had no chance for publication.

Student status in China is something special. Only 5 percent of each year's ten million high school graduates are admitted to universities. The country has 1,016 universities, about one for every million people. In contrast, the United States has 1,875 colleges and universities, or about one for every 123,000 people. It has not been easy for China to undo the damage done to education by the Cultural Revolution. During those years, 1966 to 1976, higher education nearly came to a standstill. Educators and intellectuals were persecuted.

Only in 1981 did China renew its academic degree system. It is now similar to the U.S. system, with bachelor's, master's, and doctoral degrees. For many more years the nation will continue to suffer from a severe shortage of qualified teachers and researchers in universities. Try subtracting ten years from your life and calculating the consequences.

Finally, is it possible to put these events into the context of today's China?

This nation of more than one billion persons is accustomed to taking a long view. It is, after all, one of the world's oldest continuous civilizations. And it sees itself as the "middle kingdom," which is what the word *China* refers to.

Despite periodic setbacks, the country has experienced remarkable progress under Deng Xiaoping, the nation's revered leader. An open-door policy to the rest of the world and economic and political reforms have spurred growth and development. People today are more prosperous materially than ever before. The thrust of the reforms, with the size of the population, produces change on a scale hard to grasp. It is a gigantic experiment. No one can be certain of outcomes or even where the next step will lead. You have got to admire the courage of it all.

A constant goal — and at the same time, challenge — of the leadership is to keep options open and to avoid imbalances in change across the social sector. This means pushing the accelerator here, applying the brakes there — stimulating individual enterprise while protecting job security, improving management of factories while preserving the virtues of the social system, encouraging initiative while demanding obedience, and promoting not only the economy but education.

While drawing upon the technical expertise of many different nations, the Chinese are struggling to preserve a semblance of stability for a massive development task that awaits completion — and, importantly, they are struggling to achieve the goal while maintaining the unique characteristic of what it means to be Chinese.

In China, the pendulum swings slowly, sometimes ruthlessly, always relentlessly.

9 DOUBLE ZHOUS

We'd like to stop by for a few minutes,"
one of my teaching colleagues, Zhao
Yingnan, told me over the telephone
shortly after Raija and I had settled
into Room 4605. She was calling from the security office at the entrance to the Friendship Hotel.

"All right," I said, at the same time thinking about how to entertain Chinese guests. We had tea on hand. A thermos of hot water was
always at the ready. And, luckily, we had cookies and candy.

Accompanying Zhao Yingnan, who taught the same group of
students I worked with and who holds an M.A. degree from the
University of Massachusetts, was Zhang Yijun. He was assigned to
work with me as a kind of assistant (sometimes referred to as a
waiban in Chinese).

Our two visitors were delivering a birthday cake. No one had told
them about a birthday in our family, but they had come across the
information, perhaps in the forms we had completed for our work
unit. It was a nice gesture. Atop the thick white frosting was written
Happy Birthday (in English) and the traditional wish for longevity (in
Chinese characters). This thoughtfulness and hospitality, we were to
discover, was normal treatment accorded visitors.

On November 27, Thanksgiving Day, our dining hall, responsive
to tastes and customs of the foreign guests, served turkey. The dinner
was complete with trimmings. Again, the desire to please was evident.

In December when we were in Shanghai, we were invited to two
Christmas parties. At one of them, Santa Claus distributed gifts to
youngsters. On the radio, a Shanghai station played Christmas carols,
including Gene Autry's "Rudolph, the Red-nosed Reindeer" and a
medley of his other yuletide tunes. All this was happening during the

height of the student demonstrations. Our cultural bearings were on a roller coaster.

By now, at least two things were becoming clear to Raija and me. One was the special treatment that we foreigners always received. It made us uncomfortable, especially in a land where class distinctions were supposed to be nonexistent. We remembered reading about a sign that once was posted at the entrance to Huangpu Park along Shanghai's downtown waterfront, an area called the Bund. The sign had said "Dogs and Chinese not allowed." The sign is gone, but discrimination, albeit of a different sort, continues. Worse, it is inflicted against the Chinese by the Chinese themselves. Chinese people are barred from certain shops and hotels unless accompanied by a foreigner. Chinese security officials enforce the regulation.

Why does the practice continue? We never got a good answer. To be sure, it is one way of according guests special privileges, and it is also a way to shield people from foreign visitors. We felt the Chinese we encountered were genuinely grateful for the contributions foreign experts were making to the development of their country. But there is a certain pragmatism at work here, too. In the entrepreneurial spirit of the time, many Chinese recognize that visitors represent opportunities on which to capitalize, possibly through the acquisition of foreign currency or, better yet, the cultivation of connections that might yield an educational scholarship or a chance to travel.

Just as we became aware of the special treatment accorded foreigners, Raija and I began to realize that Shanghai and Beijing are not China. The imagery of teeming throngs of people in China's cities is a distortion of the reality. Four of every five Chinese people live in rural areas. For the United States, the figures are reversed. We became more and more determined to get out of the cities and to visit other places. That becomes a bit of a challenge, though, when you are traveling on your own.

Nevertheless, Raija and I decided to leave Shanghai and take weekend trips to Hangzhou and Suzhou. The Chinese refer to the two cities, each within a few hours' train ride from Shanghai but in different directions, as the "double Zhous." The towns are two of the most popular tourist sites among the Chinese themselves. Officials often arrange meetings there, and they are favored by honeymooners. The Chinese, who probably have more aphorisms in their language than any other people, have one that reflects their sentiments about these two towns: "Above there is heaven, below there is Suzhou and Hangzhou." We were on our way to Chinese heaven.

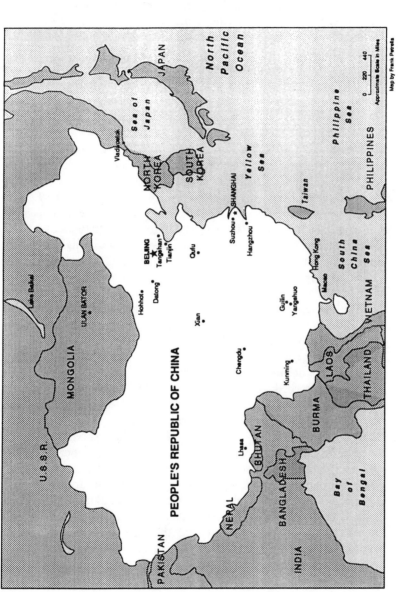

THE PEOPLE'S REPUBLIC OF CHINA

Fortunately we were traveling during the off season. The weather was less than divine in mid-December, with chilly temperatures and thick, gray clouds constantly hovering. But that was all right. Fewer people meant the towns were merely crowded — not packed. We first went to Hangzhou, a favorite retreat of Mao Zedong.

Hangzhou lies about a three-and-a-half-hour train ride southwest of Shanghai. The city of about a million permanent residents is the capital of Zhejiang Province, a region that produces one-third of China's raw silk, brocade, and satin. From the train windows you can gaze out at fertile land and peaceful countryside.

The magnet in Hangzhou is West Lake, a large freshwater lake decorated on three sides by hills and gardens. Pavilions and temples dot its banks. In early morning at this time of year, a misty veil hugs the hills, slowly dissolving into the rays of daylight. Did the French impressionists come here? Monet might have drawn the same inspiration from Hangzhou as he did from Giverny. Come to think of it, why does it matter? Culture is curious that way. In registering new information, the mind gropes for a familiar context. Thus, Westerners compare Hangzhou to Florence and Suzhou to Venice. Why not the other way around?

We had not reserved accommodations in Hangzhou because we were told it was unnecessary at this time of year. Not only did we have no trouble getting a comfortable room in the Wang Hu Hotel, but the room had a large window looking out onto the lake. Even before unpacking we decided to extend our stay.

We had learned one of the basic rules of traveling independently of a tour group in China. Upon arrival at the destination, one of the first things you must do is make arrangements to leave. You cannot make these reservations in advance. In fact, usually you have to make the reservations one day and then return another, just before departure, to pick up the tickets. It is annoying and wastes precious time. But it has one advantage: you are thrust into the cultural flow.

Hangzhou is for relaxing, walking, biking, talking. A boat ride on West Lake is mandatory. A few cents enables you to embark and disembark at various points around the lake as well as the small islands. The lake is less than four miles square. Two causeways divide

HORTATORY SIGN at West Lake in Hangzhou

the lake and make for some of the most pleasant biking up and down arched bridges in all of China.

On the boat, a young Chinese couple with two children, a boy and a girl, were eating oranges. They nonchalantly tossed the orange peelings overboard. Discarding wrappings and other such litter in this manner was a common sight. When we asked friends why people did this, the answer was, "Oh, there's someone who is supposed to pick it up." Nonetheless, around West Lake were signs in both English and Chinese on lampposts exhorting people to clean up their acts. "Everyone is committed to the promotion of public health," said one. "No spitting—a spittoon," said another, with an arrow pointing to a spittoon at the base of the lamppost. Another blended ideology and cleanliness: "Do well in sanitation—build up Socialist Civilization."

We disembarked at an island, Santanyinyue, in the middle of the lake. A city map lists the site as "Three Pools Mirroring the Moon." Presumably, on a moonlit night a series of openings placed in three hollow stone pagodas will produce three reflections of the moon on the lake.

Around West Lake and the city are other places whose physical features compete for interest with their names: Baoshu Ta (Protect Shu Tower), which overlooks the city and was built in A.D. 938 to honor Hangzhou Prince Qian Shu; Liuhe Ta (Six Harmonies Pagoda), which overlooks the Qiantang River; Lingyin Si (Temple of Inspired Seclusion), where dozens of Buddha statues have been sculpted out of a stone hillside; and Feilai Feng (Peak that Flew from Afar), which, legend says, got its name from an Indian monk who said it was just like one in India and exclaimed that it must have come from there.

A taxi ride into the countryside took us into undulating fields that rolled out like a luxurious, green carpet. As we drove slowly through a small village, a group of women standing behind makeshift wooden counters waved for us to pull over. We got out of the car, and they surrounded us. Several pulled us by our coat sleeves to their base of operation, ordered us to sit in folding camp chairs, tossed a few dark green leaves into clear glasses, added hot water from a thermos, and handed the glasses to us. It was tea, but not just any tea. The tea

A STREET CANAL in Suzhou

is famous all over China. It is called Longjing, and the women were roadside tea vendors. It was another example of modern Chinese enterprise, as well as hard sell. With this kind of welcome plus a sample, who could resist a modest purchase?

Suzhou and Hangzhou are linked by the Grand Canal, the world's longest artificial waterway, stretching more than one thousand miles from near Beijing to Hangzhou. You can travel between the double Zhous on the Grand Canal, but for us travel was easier by train.

Suzhou, east of Shanghai, is one of the oldest towns in the Yangtse River basin and has the same relaxing atmosphere as does Hangzhou. With the gardens are canals that crisscross the city and give it its distinctive character. "Garden City — Venice of the East" is Suzhou's slogan. The city is also a haven for artists.

Our travel guide — the trusty *China: A Travel Survival Kit* — suggested a hotel. With no taxis in sight, we engaged a pedicab, which has a seating compartment mounted on the back of a bicycle, to take us to the Suzhou Hotel. But first we asked about the fare.

"Fifteen *kuai,*" said the pedaler.

That amounted to about $4 U.S. The longer you are in China, the savvier you get in negotiating the price of things. In fact, for some the price becomes irrelevant. The game is the thing. The lowest possible price is the goal.

"Too much," was our response.

"Ten," he said.

That was a little more than $2.50 U.S.

He hesitated. So did we. Quite apart from any fare, just riding in a pedicab was beginning to seem too much like being transported in a rickshaw. It smacked of imperialism. While we were weighing ideology against practicality, the pedicab operator dropped the fare to eight *kuai*. That was about $2.10 U.S.

"Okay."

The trip took thirty-five minutes. It was hot. He was exhausted. And with each revolution of the pedals we felt increasing guilt over quibbling about the fare. The official practice in China is not to tip or be tipped, but both he and I ignored officialdom. So much for ideology.

After checking in at the hotel, we rented bikes from vendors in the area and, yes, headed directly back to the train station to reserve return train tickets to Shanghai.

In Suzhou you visit gardens. When Xu Zhen, vice-provost at

Fudan University and head of the university's journalism department, heard we were going to Suzhou, he insisted on drawing up a garden itinerary. Some of China's finest are here. Small enough to allow strolling around the entire grounds easily, the gardens are painstaking works of art, sculpted and manicured with stone and water as the basic working materials.

After a bird's-eye view of the city and environs from atop Bei Si (North Temple Pagoda), we headed for Zhuozheng Garden, also known as "a humble administrator's garden." On another day we visited Liuyuan (Garden for Lingering In), Wangshi (Master of Nets Garden), and others. Outside town is Tiger Hill, an entertainment center featuring dioramas showing legends of the place and a dilapidated leaning pagoda built in A.D. 961. The leaning tower is in the middle of a race between restoration and collapse.

But the real scenery around Suzhou is the ordinary: sampans plying the waterways, women doing laundry beneath a bridge, tailors and restaurateurs responding to customers in the open market in the Suzhou Bazaar, children playing with a puppy on a houseboat, workers transporting sand on a barge, a youngster tossing garbage out the back door into a canal.

Long after you've gone, Hangzhou and Suzhou tug at you. Though similar in temperament, the cities affect you differently. In Hangzhou the mountains and lake embrace you. In Suzhou you embrace the gardens and canals. They all want you to return. They did not want you to go in the first place, and leaving was a little like ending an affair.

Each morning after a 10:00 break, my students would go to their rooms on the floor above and return with their typewriters. The instruments were manual, manufactured in China, and had been issued by the students' work units. Ren Haihua, the only student from Beijing, had the only nonportable machine. She had a slight physique, and the typewriter seemed heavy enough to tip her over. We decided she should receive an unofficial academic hour of physical education credit.

The typewriters converted the classroom into an instant news laboratory. At the outset, the students carried out what I call controlled assignments. From a fact sheet or information I provided, they wrote stories. They learned quickly. Soon I imposed a time limit. Deadline pressure was a new experience for them, and some did not like it. Perhaps, I began thinking, my expectations were too high. I became lax in enforcing the deadline. That upset some students.

One who always turned his assignment in on time was Wang Keyu, twenty-nine. From Hefei City in Anhui Province, and the other half of the only couple in the class, Wang Keyu had served in the military and knew about discipline. "It's not fair," he told me, "to set a deadline and then not enforce it." He was right, of course. I adopted a firmer hand.

Before long, the students were carrying out sophisticated assignments. Outside the classroom, as part of homework, students had to develop "enterprise stories," that is, to generate their own topic ideas. They felt uncomfortable doing this, though, and much preferred being told precisely what to do. They wanted me to tell them what was right and wrong journalistically and, further, to provide models for them to follow. I refused, telling them that often it was not a matter of right and wrong but of judgment, preferably informed judgment.

76

The issue was one of educational philosophy, and I was determined to stretch their considerable talents to the limit.

Despite their initial reluctance, the students came up with topics, researched them, and produced finished stories. I discovered the stories offered me unusual windows through which to glimpse China. Subjects of their enterprise stories included the caretaker of the pandas at the Beijing Zoo, a body-building craze that was sweeping across China (prompted in part by women wearing bikinis in public), a fraudulent faith healer, a thirteen-year-old mathematics whiz, and a massage hospital run by blind people. It was not long before many of the stories they wrote began appearing in the *China Daily*.

The students always grumbled about the work I assigned. Yet once they had a clear idea of the assignments and understood the conditions, they often responded brilliantly. Though sometimes decked in unbridled flourishes of purple prose, their writing came alive with expressiveness and imagery. The grumbling somehow seemed obligatory.

Assignments occasionally involved commentary and analysis. One such assignment involved space exploration. At one time the United States National Aeronautics and Space Administration (NASA) was planning to send a journalist on a space mission. In fact, I had been a member of a national steering committee of the Association of Schools of Journalism and Mass Communication (ASJMC), which directed the Journalist-in-Space Project for NASA. Through an elaborate selection process in which every American journalist had a chance to compete, forty national finalists were chosen from among 1,795 applicants. After the Challenger disaster of January 28, 1986, the project was placed on hold by NASA and later abandoned.

Since China's space exploration program was beginning to take off, I thought it would be interesting to find out how the nation's future journalists — at least those in my class — felt about the possibility of being the first journalist in space. For while the United State's space program has been slow to recover from the Challenger setback, China has stepped up development of its program. The nation's reforms and open-door policy have helped spur its space industry. (On April 7, 1990, China launched its first foreign-built satellite, the American-made Asiasat 1. The $30-million contract, 30 to 50 percent less expensive than most American or European contracts, was handled through a consortium based in Hong Kong.)

Some Chinese, perhaps mindful that they are part of an ancient civilization, claim their space program began in the Ming dynasty around 1500. That was when a scientist named Wan Hu tied forty-seven gunpowder rockets to the back of a chair, lit the fuses, and blasted off. He died in the explosion, but his fame lives. His name is given to one of the craters of the moon in recognition of his attempt at flight. "The story also serves as further proof that the rocket was invented in China," a writer commented in an editorial-page article about China's space program in the *China Daily* (October 6, 1986).

China traces its modern space program to 1956, when the Ministry of National Defense established a department to develop missiles. Its first satellite was launched in 1970. Since then it has sent more than two dozen satellites into space with one reported failure, in 1974. Whether China's doors will ever swing wide enough to permit a journalist to board a Chinese space shuttle remains to be seen. To date, the Chinese have concentrated on unmanned space flights.

When they were asked to write an essay on the possibility of being the first journalist in space, my students saw the mission as offering a variety of opportunities, from satisfying natural curiosity to promoting the equality of women, from fulfilling journalistic responsibility to spreading peace and understanding.

Yan Xiaobin, at thirty-three, was one of the oldest in the class and greatly admired by her classmates because, besides her studies, she had to look after a one-year-old son living across town. She described what must have thrilled many Chinese in 1969 when American astronauts landed on the moon and told what they saw.

"Oh, I found it! The Great Wall!" exclaimed the native of Wuhan, Hubei Province. Projecting herself aloft, she wrote, "It looks like a gold dragon. Yes, it is a great dragon, which is the symbol of China. As a Chinese I was really impressed by the huge construction that began more than two thousand years ago."

For Zhao Shengwei, the student who commuted by crowded bus across town on weekends, the space trip would satisfy an innate need: "Man is born to explore what is strange and unknown to him, and journalists shoulder the first responsibility."

Why should a journalist go into space? Wang Xiangwei, alias Scoop, pointed out that other civilians had already made the trip. If a reporter were given a chance to fly in space, he wrote, "I think he would present us a much more accurate and vivid picture of what outer space is like."

The aspiring journalists did not ignore the potential danger of such an assignment.

"If the same tragedy should befall me," wrote Xu Yichun, the teacher from Hangzhou in Zhejiang Province whose husband was a classmate, "I would not mind being another Christa McAuliffe. To die in a significant way is much better than to live an extremely dull life. Human beings should do everything that nature has provided the chance for."

Hu Xiaohung, a former English-language teacher from Chengdu in Sichuan Province, who was usually reticent, made a similar point: "A journalist's duty is to explore new frontiers and imaginations for the public he serves. I'd like to represent millions of us all to take this adventure, to experience life out in space and thus to lead our readers' eyes outward. It's dangerous, I know. McAuliffe has already sacrificed her life, but she didn't die in vain."

Xu Yichun, perhaps thinking about the extra responsibilities Chinese society imposes on women, also saw the mission as an opportunity to help women: "Chinese women are usually considered to be inferior to the men. I want to show the world that we can do as well as men and even better."

Bian Shu, twenty-nine, a former English teacher from Hefei in Anhui Province who had been deprived of a middle-school graduation because of the Cultural Revolution, was ready to use his journalistic opportunity as an advocate for a better world: "My reports would probably deal with global pollution, excessive cutting of wood, shortage of water, and the famine in Africa." He said he would also send a message to the leaders of the United States and Soviet Union appealing for nuclear disarmament.

Among the students, peace and world understanding were the overriding themes as they contemplated story possibilities.

"The first thing I would like to do would be to write down as vividly as possible what I see and experience in outer space and call for peaceful use of outer space," wrote Zhang Xiaoquan, from the coastal city of Tianjin. She had once worked in the Chinese navy making navigation charts.

Ding Liguo continued to reflect the optimism for the future of China he had expressed in his National Day story. He wrote: "Reporting from outside earth, I would tell my fellowmen what had been beyond their reach was now at hand. I would tell them that so long as human beings did not kill each other, the world would never perish. I would tell them that the space I describe in my reporting is an inexhaustible land for man to open."

Several students were less sanguine about peace prospects in space.

"If people control space as they do on earth," wrote S. J. Peng, twenty-three, from Beng Bu City in Anhui Province, "I cannot help worrying that peaceful space will be shattered by war." Peng was a soccer-playing fanatic, and the sport helped to take his mind off the fact that his wife was back in Beng Bu.

Zou Hanru, twenty-one, from Chongqing in Sichuan Province, wrote that he would welcome the trip into space because there would be no crime, accidents, wars, or disasters. "And I hope," he continued, "that during my second trip to space, it will not be to cover a war." He did not mention food, but it was not a secret that he dearly missed the spicy dishes of his home.

Liu Shaolin, twenty-nine, also from Anhui Province, wrote of his hope that the world would become more tolerant as a result of his stories: "Through my reports, people may become aware of the values they have not yet realized. And through my exploration in space they may better understand one another and know better how to sacrifice in the interests of their fellow human beings on our globe." Truth, Liu Shaolin had told me earlier, should be the journalist's goal. "Many journalists," he said, "don't speak the truth. It is very difficult to speak the truth."

Wang (Scoop) Xiangwei had the last word on space. He was interning for *Business Weekly,* published by the *China Daily,* and was becoming socialized into the journalistic process. Already he was beginning to dislike inquisitive editors looking over his shoulder in the newsroom. He saw the trip into space as "a chance to be free for some time from the noisy city desks and sharp words uttered by irate editors."

11 NO GRANDCHILDREN

Tangshan is a thriving, modern city of more than six million, with sparkling new buildings, Western-style shopping malls, and wide thoroughfares. In the northeastern part of Hebei Province, 120 miles east of Beijing, Tangshan sits in a mineral-rich region and is, in the words of the city's vice-mayor, "the cradle of China's industrial development." The nation's first steam locomotive was built here. China's railway system began here. People have lived in the area an estimated four thousand to five thousand years. Not far away are the Eastern Tombs of the Qing dynasty (1644–1911).

But for visitors all this seems irrelevant. What matters are the six seconds that ticked agonizingly off the clock more than ten years ago and literally turned this city and the lives of its people upside down. At 3:42 a.m. Wednesday, July 28, 1976, one of the worst earthquakes in the recorded history of the world took place here. Tangshan was at the epicenter.

Nearly a quarter of a million people perished and 700,000 were injured, according to Chinese figures. That includes 148,000 in the city of Tangshan itself, which then had a population of a little over a million. Other sources say the death toll was much higher. The 1986 *World Almanac* estimates that nearly a million — the number given is eight hundred thousand — died. It is likely no one will ever know the exact number of deaths. What seems certain is that this city will exist forever under a death shroud.

Some years elapsed before the rest of the world even got an indication of the extent of the earthquake's devastation. The Chinese government refused outside offers of help. Only in February 1985 did Tangshan formally reopen its doors to the outside world.

A body count is not enough to understand this earthquake and its aftermath, for 1976 was a particularly troubled time in a nation that in this century has had its share of tremors—both political and natural. The year is cited by those who say natural calamities in China foreshadow the fall of dynasties. According to the Chinese lunar calendar, 1976 was also a year of the dragon.

Today it seems inconceivable that a disaster of the magnitude of the earthquake could be dwarfed by other events. But that is what happened. Zhou Enlai, one of the architects of modern China, died January 8, 1976. Deng Xiaoping, who today is credited with China's resurgence, was being pushed temporarily into the political shadows. The bitter end of the country's Cultural Revolution was in sight. Chairman Mao Zedong died September 9. The Gang of Four, militant leaders who had fomented the Cultural Revolution that had debilitated the nation, were arrested, later (in 1980 and 1981) to be tried, convicted, and imprisoned for plotting against the government.

Now, a decade since the earthquake, Raija and I were among a group of sixty foreign experts from sixteen different countries visiting the pleasant apartment of a husband and wife whose lives ended and began with the earthquake.

Both had been married before, each with two children. Their spouses and children died in the earthquake. The wife said she had been buried in the earthquake and was rescued by neighbors. Each left family-less by the earthquake, the woman and the man married a year later. Together they have an eight-year-old son.

"It was difficult to continue," said the gaunt woman, reaching deep inside to respond to curious visitors. "I felt very sad about the death of my family and friends." Her voice faltered. "But help from others," she struggled on, "built my confidence to continue."

The woman was near tears. We could not bring ourselves to ask more questions.

A few doors down the hall lived Bai Qian Zhong, a retired engineer, and his wife. He insisted on finding places to sit for the dozen of us who paraded through his apartment into the small living room. He passed around apples and candy and animatedly responded to questions.

"When the earthquake hit," he said, "I scrambled under the bed. Everything rocked up and down and back and forth. It lasted about six seconds. We had another tremor in the early evening. I lost my twenty-year-old son. He jumped out of the building. The building collapsed on him. I have three other sons."

He told of food delivered by plane and water and supplies transported in a caravan of one thousand cars driven from Beijing. Electricity was turned off to prevent fires. Medical stations were set up all over the city. Foreign nations offered aid, but it was refused. Chinese leaders dictated that the nation could get along without outside help.

"Are you fearful of another earthquake?" I asked.

"I'm confident that this building (he lived on the second floor of a high-rise apartment) can withstand another earthquake."

"Why wouldn't China accept help from other countries?"

"Mao said the Chinese should do it themselves."

Remains of the Tangshan earthquake can still be seen. Seven different sites have been kept as they were following the earthquake. Besides nature's monuments to its own wrath, they serve as laboratories for those studying earthquakes.

We visited the old factory of the Rolling Stock Plant, which manufactures railroad equipment. Chunks of jagged concrete and steel beams twisted like cooked spaghetti make up most of the rubble. Foliage, nature's way of healing scarred earth, was making little progress here.

Early that morning ten years ago, twenty people were on duty in the factory. Thirteen died. At that time the plant had about 7,700 workers. A total of 1,700 were killed, along with 4,000 of the workers' dependents.

In the city, 95 percent of the public buildings and just about all the homes were destroyed. The earthquake was felt in fourteen of China's twenty-one provinces.

Widespread damage occurred in Tianjin, a port city fifty miles southwest of Tangshan. Farther away in Beijing, buildings were damaged. Fearful of strong aftershocks, the government urged inhabitants of the stricken areas to eat and sleep outdoors. Tents sprang up all over, some made of plastic, others made of raincoats or umbrellas stitched together.

An American, identified by the Associated Press as Nevin Taber, an automotive engineer from Binghamton, New York, was vacationing with his family in Beijing. He remembered the jolt early that morning in their sixth floor room of the Beijing Hotel. "I felt the bed shift and I could feel the building move slowly back and forth," he said. With the electricity off, he opened the window curtains. "There were flashes of light on the horizon—either electric transformers blowing up or fires, I couldn't tell."

As a memorial, the city of Tangshan built an Earthquake Relief Monument. Its four spires stretch gracefully skyward and form a palm that looks like fingers reaching upward. A few steps away is the Exhibition Hall of the Tangshan Earthquake. Here exhibits and photographs tell the story—from the horrifying destruction to the inspiring relief effort to the amazing construction of today.

The confusion about the exact number of casualties carries over to questions about the magnitude of the quake. The Chinese say the Tangshan earthquake registered 7.8 on the Richter scale, a measure of ground motion developed in 1935. Western instruments recorded 8.2. (In comparison, the November 1988 earthquake in southwest China registered 7.6; the December 1988 Armenian earthquake, 6.9; and the 1985 Mexico City earthquake, 8.1.)

China, among all nations, has been especially prone to earthquakes. The world's two deadliest earthquakes have occurred in China, according to the *World Almanac*. The worst—an estimated 830,000 dead—took place January 24, 1556, in Shaanxi Province (once the hub of the Chinese empire and now a popular destination for tourists visiting Xian, home of the famed terra-cotta warriors). The Tangshan earthquake ranks second.

Over the years, extensive efforts have been made to forecast earthquakes, but there has been only limited success. A Chinese seismologist, Mei Shirong, director of the Earthquake Analysis and Prediction Center of the State Seismological Bureau, has advised people not to be too pessimistic or too optimistic about the forecasting. In an article in the *People's Daily*, he said there are always warning signs or indications—but "no guidelines to enable us to use them."

China has set up 460 seismological observation stations throughout the country in the past twenty years. A few earthquakes have been forecast, including one of 7.2 on the Richter scale in 1975 in Liaoning Province northeast of Beijing. The Tangshan earthquake was not predicted. Chinese scientists have identified a number of prequake indicators, including restless livestock, erratically behaving birds, and barking dogs. Since 1979, using a system of observing disturbances in well water, Chinese seismologists have forecast seven earthquakes of over 5.0 on the Richter scale.

Tangshan survivors later told of strange events they had observed one or two days before the earthquake. Water levels in wells sharply rose and fell. One factory reported that three mules refused to enter a shed. Chickens ran around chirping wildly, refusing to eat. One Tangshan resident told of a goldfish that jumped out of its tank about an hour before the earthquake struck. The owner put the goldfish back into the tank, but it jumped out again and again until the earthquake erupted.

What made our trip sad and uplifting at the same time was the human spirit of the survivors of Tangshan. We visited the Paraplegic Convalescent Hospital, one of eighteen hospitals in the city. The director, Zhang Shu Chao, told us it was built in 1979 for those who had suffered the loss of their legs. It has 204 beds and today has 115 paraplegics. The hospital has gained international attention for the way it has helped rehabilitate patients. They have learned to speak foreign languages, to write for newspapers or magazines, to operate a grocery. Some make up a musical troupe consisting entirely of performers confined to wheelchairs. They presented a concert for us, and tears could not be restrained when twenty-three-year-old Dong Mei sat proudly in her wheelchair and sang.

On the outskirts of Tangshan we visited a care center for the earthquake's oldest and youngest victims — the elderly who lost families in the disaster and the earthquake orphans. We were invited into modest homes. A seventy-six-year-old woman, her feet made tiny by binding (an old Chinese custom now abandoned), leaned forward on a cane. She had lost her entire family. She told her story simply and sadly: "If it were not for the earthquake, I would be a grandmother today." The gravity of the comment registers only if you have some notion of the closeness of Chinese family ties and how parents in their old age depend on their adult children.

The young children orphaned by the earthquake numbered 4,200. Some babies had just been born, and the earthquake left them without names.

For some reason, our interest in the earthquake could not be satiated. Even at the magnificent new Ceramics Exhibition Center, talk turned to the earthquake. The Center director, Zhao Yonghe, remembered he had gone to bed late on the night of July 27.

"It had been very hot. I was sound asleep. The earth suddenly moved. I awoke and found myself buried."

His family was also buried, but all were rescued.

"What happened to the ceramics factory?"

"Everything was destroyed. A new factory was rebuilt in another location."

"Was it difficult to go on?"

"The people of Tangshan felt very strongly about the need to rebuild."

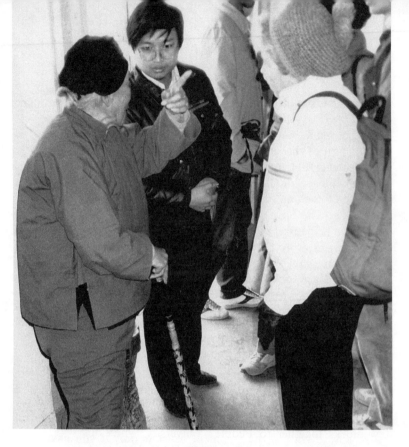

FOREIGN VISITORS meet a care center
resident in Tangshan.

A popular book about the earthquake has been written by
Chinese journalist Qian Gang. Titled *The Great China Earthquake,* it
has been published in English by the Foreign Languages Press of
Beijing.

While visitors are eager to learn about the earthquake, the city
strives to look forward. The city's vice-mayor, Long Jiajun, met with
us and told how Tangshan has come back from the ruins. Indeed, an
entirely new city has been built.

"We still have problems and hardships after the ten years," he
said. "For example, the industrial pollution—it's as bad now as before. But," he continued, "at least now our city has a very bright
future."

By any standards, the rise of Tangshan from the rubble represents a triumph of human cooperation, resiliency, and courage. To us
it seemed a symbol of a similar, even greater challenge confronting all
of contemporary China—the rebuilding of an entire nation.

12 FOUR "BIGS"

Apowdery snow glistened against the streetlights along Baishiqiao Road as Raija and I walked with Zhao Shengwei, one of my students, to his home on the People's University campus. It was the evening of New Year's Day 1987. We had tried to get together before, during National Day, but the usual cross-cultural scourge—miscommunication, for lack of a better term—had him waiting at one place while Raija and I were walking blithely and ignorantly in another direction. This time Zhao Shengwei came directly to the hotel entrance. We strolled the few blocks together to People's University, where his wife taught. They lived on campus in a large one-room apartment for faculty and staff.

It was a good time and place to begin 1987. The new year marked the fifteenth anniversary of the renewal of ties between the United States and China. Officials from the two nations were exchanging friendly visits, recalling the day when President Richard Nixon dramatically set foot on Chinese soil. My memory played back old television images: Nixon shaking hands with Chairman Mao Zedong, Nixon at the banquet in the Great Hall of the People, Nixon at the Great Wall, and thousands of Chinese with brooms sweeping a light snow from the streets to clear a path for the visiting Americans. At the time, the pictures seemed stranger than those of Americans walking on the moon.

The significance of Nixon's journey cannot be exaggerated. The event signaled growing economic and cultural ties between the two nations. It drove a diplomatic wedge between the United States and Taiwan. It ended a long period of international hibernation for mainland China. Though Nixon's first visit to China took place February 21–28, 1972, it was to be seven years, January 1, 1979, before

87

the two nations formally established diplomatic relations.

At the Zhaos' apartment, we enjoyed warmth from the charcoal briquettes smoldering in the small stove in the middle of the room as well as from the joint enterprise of stuffing *jiaozi* (dumplings). The production of dumplings in the preparation of a meal is a social activity drawing family and friends together. The Zhaos' energetic two-year-old son provided additional entertainment.

Conversation turned to Nixon and the student demonstrations of the past month. Zhao Shengwei shared the sentiments of most Chinese in his unrestrained praise for the former president. Watergate is not part of the Chinese image of the man. As for the student demonstrations, Zhao Shengwei described the Chinese media's coverage as "one-sided." I did not have to ask for additional explanation. But what really excited Zhao Shengwei was his showing us several prized family possessions: a refrigerator, a washing machine, and a color television set. Thriftiness, diligence, and hard work were paying off. Are these values Western? Eastern? Capitalistic? Socialistic?

The trip to my student's home suggested an undercurrent in the modest fifteenth-anniversary observance. While U.S. and Chinese officials talked about improved relations in the last decade and a half and expressed hope for even closer ties in the future, both nations were preoccupied with their own domestic affairs. In the United States, it was the Iran-Contra affair. In China, it was the continuing fallout from the student demonstrations and the impact on domestic changes.

The preoccupation with internal affairs became evident during the visit in March 1987 of the U.S. secretary of state, George Shultz. He came to mark the anniversary of the Shanghai Communiqué, which had laid the groundwork for United States–Chinese ties. Chinese leader Deng Xiaoping spoke with him about the "small troubles" of President Ronald Reagan. He added that the Chinese had similar difficulties. The Chinese news agency Xinhua quoted Deng Xiaoping as saying, "As for the recent troubles [student demonstrations], they are over. But maybe they will exist for a long time in the minds of the people."

Despite official cordialities, the fact remains that China and the United States take a guarded view of each other. Living and working in China make you appreciate the sentiments on both sides.

On the one hand, Chinese officials want to assure the United States that the door really is open, despite occasional chilly gusts such as the attacks on "bourgeois liberalization." On the other hand,

ELEMENTARY SCHOOL CHILDREN
happily perform for visitors in Qing Pu
County near Shanghai.

American diplomats express concern and even consternation over the
assaults against so many things decidedly Western. The Chinese want
Western technology and the incentives of the economic system. But
they do not want what they call the social pollutants — crime, pornog-
raphy, corruption, etc. — that they associate with Western democra-
cies. The link between democracy and morality may be tenuous, but
you cannot fault the concern.

The United States, meanwhile, argues that the Chinese cannot
selectively import American know-how and at the same time condemn
the source and the system. The Chinese want it both ways.

In remarks to a group of us Fulbright professors meeting in
January 1987 in Kunming, the U.S. ambassador to China, Winston
Lord, said that an enormous effort is required in "trying to understand these two vastly different societies." Ambassador Lord accompanied President Nixon and national security adviser Henry Kissinger
on the 1972 mission. He knows about the two cultures. It is difficult
and challenging to build economic ties and encourage exchange pro-

grams, but it helps bridge the cultural gap, enriching both cultures in the process.

Since its Cultural Revolution, China has accomplished a social and economic miracle through a variety of reforms. The ten-year-long nightmare had devastated the nation's economy as well as the people's morale. There was only one direction to go, and that was up. The bumpy road toward modernization has become even more difficult for several reasons, all domestic: the desire for continued economic growth, the need to maintain stability during a leadership transition, and the consequences of Hong Kong's coming under Chinese rule.

Early successful reforms, particularly those fostering free markets, have led to a stage of development in which changes become more uncertain and even less identifiable. Previous game plans must be revised constantly to take into account new factors, including such spontaneous events as student unrest. The Chinese do not want to jeopardize economic progress. If anything, the goal is to continue developing the economy in the interest of overall nation building. To date, China has made the most of its opportunities, building domestic stability while engendering confidence abroad. In China's cities and villages, visitors see vitality that borders on the inspirational.

In December we visited a town, Xu Jin, in Qing Pu County on the outskirts of Shanghai. A town official, Zhang Weihui, told how, as a result of reforms, the community shifted its focus from agriculture to manufacturing. Residents benefited from improved social services, and their annual per capita income from 1978 to 1985 doubled to 852 *yuan* ($230 U.S.). In 1987 the figure was expected to reach 1,550 *yuan* ($419 U.S.). This was extraordinary in a nation where urban residents had annual incomes of about 1,000 *yuan* ($270 U.S.) and per capita income in rural areas — where eight hundred million of China's billion-plus people live — was a little more than 400 *yuan* ($108 U.S.).

A gauge of how the Chinese standard of living has changed is the shift in the demand for goods. In the 1960s people wanted watches, sewing machines, and bicycles. Today they want the four "bigs": color television sets, double-cassette tape recorders, double-door refrigerators, and twin-tub washing machines. You can understand student Zhao's enthusiasm. He and his family were on the way to prosperity.

We could see another reminder of rapid growth by looking out the northwest corner of our sixth-floor apartment in the Friendship Hotel. One spring day, I counted twelve giant cranes working at twelve separate construction sites. "City birds," urbanites describe

WORKERS UNLOAD while prospective buyers inspect newly arrived refrigerators along Xuanwumennei Street in downtown Beijing.

them with a smile. The scenes were repeated throughout China. But keeping the economy moving is a major problem, especially cultivating the private sector on which the Chinese pin high hopes. Despite its growth, private business employs only about 1 percent of the nation's official 476-million-strong work force. Toward the end of our year, the government was trying to deal with two other economic problems—inflation and widespread corruption among officials.

Another major concern in the continuing development of the nation is a smooth leadership transition. Deng Xiaoping, the dominant leader of China since his return to power in 1977, searched for years for someone to take the helm and carry on the reform movement. Deng's plans suffered a setback in early 1987 when Hu Yaobang was forced to resign as general secretary of the Communist party in the aftermath of the 1986–1987 student demonstrations. (Hu Yaobang's death April 15, 1989, at the age of seventy-three set off more widespread demonstrations, culminating June 4 in what has come to be known outside China as the Tiananmen Massacre and inside China as the Tiananmen Incident.) He and Deng had been associates for forty years, and Hu was widely believed to be Deng's successor. The first major step in leadership change came at the party's thirteenth Central Committee Meeting, held November 2, 1987, when Zhao Ziyang was elected general secretary of the Chinese Communist party. Deng's influence as paramount leader, though, was hardly diminished. He retained several key posts, including that of chairman of the Military Commission of the party's Central Committee.

China's continuity of leadership, of course, comes from the Communist party. By way of maintaining its primary role in governance, it has exhorted people, more than before, to adhere to the four principles: the socialist road, the people's democratic dictatorship, the leadership of the Communist party, and Marxism-Leninism-Mao Zedong thought. The leadership question is closely linked to the next turn in China's future. If hard-line conservatives gain the upper hand, then China, in the estimation of much of the world, will take a big step backward.

Another important domestic factor in China's future is resumption of the sovereignty over Hong Kong, scheduled to take place officially in 1997. It will be a supreme test-tube case of mating sharply differing ideologies. The Basic Law Drafting Committee has drawn up a blueprint for the territory's constitution after 1997 (the document was made public in May 1988). Hong Kong, as only a brief visit to that bustling metropolis will attest, epitomizes "bourgeois liberalism." The whole world will be watching the way China implements its promise of "one nation, two systems."

The press, of course, is one barometer to watch. The Hong Kong media enjoy a robust, aggressive journalism, the kind respected newspapers in the West practice. In early 1987, as part of the effort to curb "bourgeois liberalization," China established a Media and Publications Office to control various aspects of publishing and news operations throughout the country. At the same time, the Communist party expelled from its ranks the country's most famous journalist, Liu Binyan, who had gained great national popularity as a muckraking journalist for the *People's Daily.*

Restrictions on press freedom in Hong Kong would appear to be a distinct possibility, although the "one nation, two systems" policy does call for Hong Kong to retain its present legal system after 1997. At the very least, press freedom, as Hong Kong journalists now define it, will face its stiffest test. The present climate for change on the mainland suggests that the unification of Hong Kong and China will have repercussions in both directions. Hong Kong could have an important impact on China, particularly in the realm of industry and commerce.

A humorous story told by one of my students illustrates how far China's economy has come and how far the entrepreneurial spirit has gone. It was written by Zhou Fang, twenty-six, who worked as a translator for the Coal Plant Design Institute in Henan Province before beginning his journalism studies. The story is about a fish vendor.

"Hello! Hello! Please buy my live fish. Come and see how fresh they are."

Guang (not his complete name) is busy selling fish. He greets every passerby and boasts of the freshness of his fish.

Since 1983 thousands of private fish vendors have popped up in Beijing.

People living here can enjoy fresh fish at low prices. Selling fish turns a good profit. This attracts many young people. Guang is one of them.

The day I visited him he was selling his fish near Ditan Park (Temple of Earth) in the northeastern part of the city. He looked vigilant when I interviewed him. He mistook me as a tax collector. He was relaxed after I showed him my identification.

"You see, I don't have a stationary stand. My bike serves as a stand. My home is in Tongxian County. I have a fish pond which I dug two years ago. I have to get up every morning at 3:00 or 4:00 and ride to the city.

"I was a farmer before I sold fish. I was poor then. But now I'm rich. I earn about 500 *yuan* ($135 U.S.) a month. I will replace my bike with a motorcycle."

Asked why he did not have a permanent site for his business, he looked around and then told me in a low voice: "I don't want to pay a tax."

As so often happens, it was difficult to distinguish between a culturally universal trait or one that was culturally distinctive. Maybe resistance to taxes is something culturally instinctive.

13   LOCOMOTIVE CITY

In a rapidly changing nation like China, anachronisms are commonplace. One day on a tour of the *People's Daily,* I saw the latest in computer equipment being installed. A few days earlier at Xinhua, I had seen half a dozen workers scurrying up and down and back and forth along a tunnellike corridor lined on both sides with cases. They were setting type — by hand. Like plucking flowers in an elongated garden, the compositors were gathering Chinese characters etched into pieces of metal and wood. Together the pieces would form a sentence or headline of printed type.

I paused to take a photograph of the workers assembling their "bouquets" of type. Our guide intervened.

"No photos allowed here."

I put the camera away. As a guest, I was not about to offend unnecessarily. Perhaps in some other circumstance, I might be able to justify being offensive. But not here. Under my breath, I was muttering about the reason for the photo prohibition since I knew Xinhua, which employs some five thousand persons and operates more than one hundred bureaus throughout China and the world, also has the latest in computer composition equipment. I had even taken photos of it. No one had objected then.

The young man from Anhui Province who had been assigned by my work unit to assist and look after me said, in reference to the hand composition, "It's old. It might be embarrassing."

From my standpoint, there was no reason for embarrassment. New is not necessarily better. Setting type by hand surely is cumbersome and inefficient. Yet there is a sense of self-involvement and permanence that the transience of a computer screen cannot match.

A historical irony for a China struggling toward modernization is that some of the world's most significant inventions have occurred in China. These include the so-called four inventions: paper, printing, gunpowder, and the magnetic compass. Long before the West succeeded, as early as the Tang dynasty (618–907), the Chinese had invented printing.

Why did not China exploit for its own developmental purposes the scientific inventions and discoveries that changed much of the rest of the world? It is a good question. It haunted me as Raija and I entered another time warp, this time on a journey to the last place in the world where steam-engine locomotives were produced.

A coal-dust halo loomed over the town of Datong as our overnight train from Beijing pulled into the station about noon on a cold January morning. Blackness had settled into our clothing and hair. I tried unsuccessfully to rub the soot and sleep from my eyes. Even the wind-whipped snowflakes swirling across town were tainted with black specks. Our lodging — surely the only hotel in the world with the name Locomotive Works Guest House — had a coal-mining decor. And the food seemed to have grit for seasoning.

But none of that mattered. We — Raija and I, and Fran Somers and Larry Johnson, the couple who worked for *China Reconstructs,* a Beijing-based magazine published in several languages — were at a hallowed spot. For those who remember and love trains powered by steam, this is Mecca. Datong is home to the world's last steam-engine locomotive plant that produced full-size locomotives on a regular basis. Except perhaps for hobbyists, the manufacturing of steam-engine locomotives would seem to be a step back in time. For China it was merely the application of appropriate technology in the nation's particular stage of development.

The reason? "Low costs and ease of use," explained Liu Kun Shun, an official for the Datong Locomotive Factory who is practiced at giving short, direct answers to such questions. He had joined the factory at its beginning thirty years ago and had come up through the ranks as a welding technician.

The low production costs depend on Datong's location. The city, an overnight train ride west of Beijing, is in China's biggest coal-producing province, Shanxi. Steel is readily available from the bordering province of Inner Mongolia. The barren loess lands around Datong are those that appear in the award-winning Chinese film *Yellow Earth.* The town itself, noted Mr. Liu, is near two major railway hubs, Beijing and Taiyuan. Outdoors, in the freezing temperature, men in fur caps and padded garments gazed somberly ahead as they guided their horses and mules pulling two-wheeled wooden carts loaded with coal from the Heng Mountains into Datong.

"There are disadvantages (to steam locomotives)," Mr. Liu told us from behind his dark, horn-rimmed glasses. Again he was succinct: "Poor efficiency and pollution."

Efficiency involves calorific (heat-producing) levels. Thirty percent of the energy generated by the steam engine literally goes up in smoke. Heat escapes through a chimney.

A major research project at the factory was being carried out by David Wardale, one of a vanishing breed of steam-engine experts. He had gone from England to South Africa and now, for a three-year assignment, to Datong. His task was to design a more efficient engine for the medium-size locomotive. The factory produced its first engine in 1959. Since then more than 5,000 steam locomotives have come through its cavernous facilities. It took fifty-two days to make a locomotive from start to end, Liu said. The annual output was 325, although the number in 1987 had dropped to 272. The decline may have been due to political and economic turmoil. But visitors like us and the twenty-five hundred tourists who come every year to the factory do not help either.

"We've had to limit visits to Tuesdays and Saturdays," he said. "Otherwise it interferes with production."

Lucky for us, our visit was on a Saturday. That meant we got to tour two huge buildings that sprawl over several square blocks where the locomotives are made. They are Brobdingnagian blacksmith shops.

Donning plastic protective helmets, we walked the womb of the steam-locomotive factory. We started with raw steel and moved on to lathes, welders, boilers, pistons, fire bins, wheels, cabs. Sparks flew. Light flashed. Metal clanged against metal. In half an hour we had traversed the entire production process. Men and women, not machines, seemed to do most of the work. It looked primitive, even dangerous for the workers.

Of course, the work actually had begun with a design. Originally this was provided by the Russians. But since then several other de-

NEAR THE END of the assembly process, a steam locomotive emerges at the Datong Locomotive Factory.

ENGINEER TAO RUNG proudly takes a new steam-engine locomotive for a test drive.

signs had been adapted, and the Chinese claimed them as their own.

The climax of the factory tour was a test drive of the factory's latest issuance—engine number QJ 7167. The initials are Chinese for *Qian Jin*—Marching Forward—and they denote an engine class. The factory's other major class is JS, for *Jian She,* meaning Reconstructs. Engineer Tao Rung was at the controls. We were cabin passengers. Engineer Tao's pride in this shiny black beauty with red wheels seemed to hiss outward like the white bursts of steam in the cold January air. The test ride took about a minute and covered about fifty yards. When it was over, QJ 7167 presumably was ready to hit the rails. We felt a little more testing might be called for but went along with the fillip to tourists.

The factory has 9,335 employees, 2,800 of them women. There are 400 engineers and technicians. Nearly all live in factory quarters, creating a "locomotive city." It has a 2,300-seat theater, educational facilities from nursery to college, a 130-bed hospital, parks, shops, and the Locomotive Works Guest House. It was another example of a minisociety organized around the work unit. "It is a community to itself," affirmed Liu. The city of Datong has 800,000 inhabitants.

"What of the future of the steam-engine locomotive in China?" I asked. Liu was blunt. The move is toward diesel. The factory produces some diesel engines and is experimenting with gas-driven engines. The diesel engines cost more but produce more power and less pollution, he said. For the present, China's railway system is powered half by steam and half by diesel. That ratio will change drastically in the next few years. For on December 21, 1988, the plant produced its last steam-engine locomotive, and production shifted to diesel and electric engines.

Mr. Liu told us the factory was not in the export business. But an American organization of railroad enthusiasts called the Boone and Scenic Valley Railroad purchased at a cost of $355,000 one of the last steam locomotives to be produced in Datong. The engine arrived in the central Iowa town of Boone in early December 1989, where it is now chugging along as a tourist attraction.

Meanwhile, China has taken steps to preserve the lore of the vanishing steam-powered train. The government has designated a refuge for steam locomotives in the northernmost province of Heilongjiang. It will be the last province in China to give them up.

The last city to use steam engines, according to the *China Daily* (March 21, 1987), will be Jiamusi, three hundred miles northeast of Harbin, in Heilongjiang. Jiamusi, a city of half a million, is literally to become a living steam-locomotive museum. Some of the locomotives being assembled in Heilongjiang were manufactured in China before 1949. Others are old Japanese products. Still older locomotives come from Britain, Germany, the United States, Poland, and Finland.

The locomotive factory is not the city's main attraction, except, of course, for the railroad buffs. For others, the place to visit is the Yungang Caves. Built into the side of Wuzhou Mountain ten miles to the west, the caves contain more than fifty thousand statues that represent some of the oldest examples of stone sculpture in China. Also outside of town, about forty-five miles away, is the Hanging Monastery, a fourteen-hundred-year-old structure clinging halfway up the precipice of Jinlong Canyon. The city also has a Mass Graves Exhibition Hall, a grim reminder of how in the 1930s Japanese troops executed Chinese people and exploited the coal mines.

As we made the train trip back to Beijing on Sunday afternoon, the question we had begun the trip with returned: Why had the Chinese been unable to exploit their own inventions and discoveries? Many scholars, including Joseph Needham, one of the most eminent authorities on science in China, have pondered the question. No one seems to have the answer.

The question came up at a Beijing symposium called "Continuity and Change: The Past in China's Present." One of three speakers, Professor Liang Congjie, suggested the answer has less to do with the use of science and technology and more to do with the use of information and knowledge. A sociologist of science at the Encyclopedia of China Publishing House, Professor Liang is studying the classification of knowledge in early encyclopedias from China and the West. The ways in which the two cultures classify knowledge reflect different ways of thinking, he said. The West has its tree of knowledge, suggesting continuing growth and interrelationships of the known. China's depiction of the known, on the other hand, can be illustrated as a series of concentric circles representing human relationships. The seat of authority—presumably the emperor—occupied the innermost seat of knowledge. People on the outer edge of the circle had the least access to knowledge, while those close to the center had the greatest access to knowledge. According to Professor Liang's argument, communication of information spread out along the branches in the West in contrast to being controlled at the center in China.

Professor Liang's thesis had other facets. For example, while the West tamed nature, China sought an integration of people and nature. In the West, individuals made discoveries and wrote books, while in

China these endeavors were carried out by groups of individuals working under a ruler. I did not fully understand Professor Liang's argument, but his ideas offered some fresh paths toward probing the global impact of culture on human behavior and understanding. Professor Liang's thesis, as one might expect, is controversial. No doubt other explanatory factors, such as social and economic conditions as well as political structures, figure in national development. But each of these factors would seem to have its own communication and information component.

By now our train was nearing Beijing. From the windows, looking up, we could see a section of the Great Wall. Minutes later we arrived at the teeming train station. Thoughts of printing blocks and steam engines evaporated in the usual struggle to survive among the jostling crowds.

14   FUTURE AS PAST

Change suggests something unfolding, developing, moving forward. That is not an adequate conception. Change is not just what lies ahead but also our changing notion of what lies behind. In China change seems to take place every bit as quickly backward as forward. While the Chinese move toward the twenty-first century, they are busily exploring a heritage unrivaled among the nations of the world.

Almost daily, archaeologists unearth new and fascinating discoveries. The following "finds" were made during a few months in the fall of 1986:

Nearly one thousand relics, items made of bronze, lacquer, and bamboo, including weapons and musical instruments, were recovered from a tomb in Jiangling County, Hubei Province. The items are believed to be twenty-three hundred years old.

In the Xinjiang Uygur Autonomous Region, Chinese archaeologists discovered more than fifty well-preserved mummies dating from more than three thousand years ago.

Archaeologists in northern China's Shaanxi Province discovered the ruins of a two-thousand-year-old army outpost. It is believed to have been home to several thousand soldiers.

In Yuhang County, Zhejiang Province, archaeologists uncovered a group of tombs dating back more than four thousand years.

Stone-age artifacts and the fossilized remains of more than thirty

AT XIAN in Shaanxi Province, vendors sell replicas of the famed terra-cotta warriors and horses.

animal species were found in a cave in Wuxuan County in south China's Guangxi Zhuang Autonomous Region.

More than one thousand bronze statues were excavated in Guanghan County in southwest China's Sichuan Province. They date back three thousand years.

The list could go on. And of course it will. Even visitors who have a full year in China must confine themselves to a mere sampling of the country's dazzling attractions. But perhaps no historical-cultural relic is more magnetic than the group of terra-cotta warriors in the dusty countryside of Xian in Shaanxi Province, about six hundred miles southwest of Beijing. It is the cradle of Chinese civilization — China's equivalent of the Acropolis and the pyramids. Here backward and forward change have meshed in such a way that the ancient warriors of the past would be no match for the troops who now patrol the souvenir front. Just outside the entrance gates to the terra-cotta warrior museum, where legions of hawkers stalk unwary gawkers, this scene is common:

"Duo shao qian?" (How much money?) Raija asked a middle-aged woman. She pointed at a nine-inch-high kneeling archer.

"Er shi wu."

On a slip of paper, Raija wrote 25 to be sure (25 *yuan* equals $6.75 U.S.).

The woman, in padded jacket and pants, nodded yes.

"Tai gui le" (too much), Raija said confidently. She had had the benefit of consumer counsel from other members of the traveling group.

Raija looked off toward another vendor.

"How much you pay?" countered the woman in broken English, seeing a potential sale slipping away.

Raija: *"San kuai, wu mao,"* in even more broken Chinese (3.50 *yuan* equals about $.94 U.S.).

The woman: *"Er shi"* (20 *yuan*).

Pause.

The woman, now more determined: *"Shi wu"* (15 *yuan*).

Pause. Raija shuffled her feet.

The woman: *"Shi"* (10 *yuan*).

Raija: *"Wu"* (5 *yuan*).

Agreed.

The price was about $1.35 in U.S. currency.

The buying and selling going on here was toe-to-toe warfare, with no holds barred. Sometimes after a bargain was struck, the merchant tried to substitute a lesser item. Tourists who had made their way to this part of the world could not be all that concerned over a few dollars. Something else was going on. The object's intrinsic value was only part of what was at stake. Equally involved were ego and competition and personal gain. Capitalism.

The prices of the replicas of the warriors and horses — as well as the prices of slides, postcards, and vests — are highly variable and, by American standards, low. But the business of selling tourists souvenirs is anything but small change. In Lintong County, where the warriors are located, more than one hundred thousand country women in 1986 earned a total of 32 million *yuan* ($8.6 million U.S.) selling products ranging from small replicas of terra-cotta figures to mandarin jackets, according to Xinhua. In recent years the number of tourist products has multiplied from ten varieties to more than four hundred. The size of the selling battlefield had more than tripled since my first visit in the fall of 1984. It was clear that these modern mercenaries of the marketplace have pinned their hopes for the future on a recovery of the past.

More than a million visitors come to Xian each year. They include presidents, queens and kings, prime ministers, and just about anyone who wants to make a visit to China complete. Ronald Reagan bought a red mandarin jacket in Xian. Queen Elizabeth had walked among the sculpted warriors just two months before Raija and I made the trip with a group of foreign experts on an overnight train ride from Beijing. Though I had been here before, the awe remained.

Xian is much more than the terra-cotta warriors, however. Many sites in and around the city offer glimpses into the evolution of China's culture. The Forest of Stelae, part of the Shaanxi Provincial Museum, is one such place. It is a library, a "forest of books," consisting of engraved stone tablets — many standing taller than a person — that record China's history and culture. Some of the Chinese language's finest calligraphy is preserved here. The library contains twenty-three hundred engraved stone tablets and encompasses a two-thousand-year period, with the earliest tablets dating from the Han dynasty (206 B.C.–A.D. 220). Centuries ago this method of carving into stone must have represented a dramatic technological breakthrough. I wondered if people at the time thought of it as high tech. Artisans today use a soft mallet to tap onion-skin paper held up to the stone carving to reproduce messages from the past. The results are called rubbings and are popular souvenirs.

Another place worthy of a visit is the Banpo Neolithic Village, an

on-site museum containing the ruins of a six-thousand-year-old village and representing the earliest signs of human habitation around
Xian. Discovered in 1953, the village is believed to have been organized at one time around a matriarchal society. In front of the
entrance is a statue of a huge, bare-breasted, pregnant woman, which
leaves no doubt as to who was in charge.

Strolling through the museums and reading the occasional English-language placard, Raija and I were struck by the sprinkling of
ideology into the explanatory signs. A placard at a moat at the Banpo
Museum tells of the "inhabitants' determination to overcome natural
difficulties by working together." Another sign refers to a Communist
society — six thousand years ago. Another mentions that this society
did not prosper because only a classless society can be highly produc-
tive. It occurred to us that this is what happens everywhere in the
world. How can you separate interpretation of the past from the
ideology of the present? The past is more fluid than we realize.

The museums in Xian and other places we visited in China are
not maintained very well. We saw thousand-year-old relics housed in
display cases with the glass broken. You could have reached in and
removed an object. The sculpture outdoors, much like the statuary at
the Acropolis in Greece, is eroding. The culprits are clear: industrial
pollution, harsh weather, outright looting, and simple wear and tear.
Solutions require money, and there is not enough available. China's
officials face the enormous challenge of accelerating opportunities for
restoring the treasure-trove of the past and pressing demands for its
continuing maintenance.

Other sites in and around Xian compete for attention: the City
Walls, among the few original walls of any city to be found in China;
the Big Goose and Little Goose pagodas, temples in which Buddhist
scriptures were preserved and which now offer panoramic views of the
countryside; the Great Mosque, one of the largest Islamic mosques in
China; and Huaqing Pool, hot springs located at the base of a mountain and perhaps best known for the so-called Xian Incident of 1936,
when Chiang Kaishek was arrested by his own generals and was
forced to participate in the resistance against the Japanese.

But the terra-cotta warriors are the pièce de résistance. We got
there late in the morning after a thirty-minute bus ride from Huaqing
Pool. Along the way, sandy, dark-brown soil and red-brick and mud
buildings suggested nothing extraordinary. Horse-drawn buggies
slowed the traffic. There is some farming, though not much, for the

land is harsh. It is easy to imagine that the peasants who were digging in this area about eighteen miles east of Xian in 1974 must have been disappointed at not finding the water they were looking for. What they turned up was one of the greatest archaeological finds in the world.

Our narrow blacktop road widened after the last turn, and there was the place, a plain building with a curved roof, looking like an oversized athletic facility. We walked into the building and immediately faced hundreds of warriors, some armed with spears and dagger-axes, others with crossbows.

The eleven rows of warriors and horses, separated by mounds of earth, appear to be in trenches. As we looked toward the rear lines, we saw dismembered bodies—a head lying here, a body there, limbs strewn around. Some warriors were still emerging from the earth. The warriors have survived a grim battle, one that has lasted more than two thousand years. Each figure is exquisitely done. Each differs in features and expressions. Each has been sculpted in the appropriate fighting garb of the day. Each is positioned in accordance with an ancient book on the art of war.

Inside are signs saying no photographs are allowed. Some over-zealous shutterbugs, we are told, have had film confiscated. Yet the urge is irresistible. At waist-high level and with available light, I snapped the shutter of my automatic-focus camera several times. A hand tapped me on the right shoulder. It belonged to a uniformed guard. Chagrined, I was prepared to suffer the consequences. My guilt was obvious. So perhaps was my remorse. The guard merely shook his head and finger sideways in an unspoken language anyone can understand.

Separate museum buildings nearby tell the story of the warriors. The huge necropolis was built by the first emperor of a unified Chinese people, Qin Shihuang (259–210 B.C.). The emperor is remembered for some amazing accomplishments: building the Great Wall for defense purposes, standardizing weights and measures, building roadways. But, as our guide said, "He was also cruel and people did not live well."

"Cruel" was being kind. As was the custom of the day, work began on the emperor's tomb at the start of his rule. In Qin Shihuang's case, the effort reached an unprecedented scale and lasted more than thirty-five years of his reign. The tomb is said to have contained palaces and elaborate furnishings of gold and silver. After the emperor was buried, the artisans and palace maids who had no children were buried alive in the underground tomb so that its secrets would be preserved.

In one exhibit, a placard beside a builder's bleached bones read: "They were thrown into the tomb without any funerary objects. This truthfully reflects the heavy corvées [unpaid labor extracted by authorities] and the cruel class oppression in the Qin Dynasty."

The museum is not finished. According to one count, there are 714 life-size warriors and horses. Their numbers are multiplying through excavation. By 1990 the museum may have a total of three thousand figures on display. The museum may never be finished.

Uncovering the past is never ending. In China the past unfolds every bit as rapidly as the future.

III
三

15 BOURGEOIS
PROFESSOR

W hen spring semester began in late February, I was apprehensive about reentering the classroom. Since the student demonstrations in December and January, the rhetoric about "bourgeois liberalism" had been turned up to fever pitch. During the semester break from January to February, we, as newcomers to China, were seeing evidence of the backlash by authorities that had been predicted by veteran observers of such events.

During the vacation, Raija and I had traveled in the warm climes of southeast Asia. We had managed to keep up with some of the developments within China, and the news was increasingly disturbing. An American journalist, Lawrence MacDonald, working for the French news agency, Agence France-Presse, was accused of obtaining information from a Chinese student and was expelled from China. The use of such a source was not unusual, since Western correspondents always found it difficult to get information from other than governmental sources. We knew of correspondents who had paid Chinese students to report on events at their campuses. MacDonald's expulsion apparently was intended to serve as an example for other correspondents.

In the assault on bourgeois liberalism, several prominent intellectuals had been purged from the Communist party. One was Liu Binyan, China's most prominent investigative journalist and a professional idol of my students. In addition, a new agency, the Media and Publications Office, had been created to supervise all aspects of the nation's publishing and news operations.

We wondered what impact all this would have on my teaching

during the second semester. How would it affect my relationship with the students? The relationship had moved from one of mutual formality and wariness to one of geniality and trust. We had succeeded in creating a constructive learning atmosphere. Now, in light of an apparent clampdown, might the class itself be threatened and the rest of the academic year be abandoned? Would it even be safe to return to China?

Another incident, which had occurred in the classroom near the end of the first semester, also had disturbed me. It involved cheating, the only such case I detected the entire year. It grew out of an official visit to China by the U.S. secretary of defense, Caspar Weinberger. The U.S. Embassy had set up a press office on the tenth floor of the Minzu Hotel next to the Nationalities Cultural Palace. I managed to arrange a tour of the facilities and a briefing for my students. For most students, this was a totally new experience. Some had never before been inside a hotel such as the Minzu, which catered to foreign visitors. Later, as homework, I gave each student a transcript of a speech Weinberger had delivered at the University of National Defense in Beijing. Their task was to write an account of the speech and to bring it to the next class meeting.

In evaluating the students' work, I noticed one story sounded ominously familiar. I had seen it elsewhere. I checked several sources, and there it was: an account of the speech that Xinhua had transmitted over its wire service. The student's account and that of Xinhua were identical. How to deal with this? Should I notify institute officials? I suspected they would prefer being notified and would be greatly embarrassed and angry. But I decided to handle the matter in the same way as I would in the States. I asked the student to come to my office after class. I showed the student the two copies of the story. The student offered no excuses, was very apologetic, and said it would not happen again. We discussed the importance of professional and individual integrity. I gave the student a failing grade for the paper and, given the student's apology, decided one indiscretion was permissible.

In discussions with other American teachers later, I discovered they too occasionally came across instances of cheating. One reason for cheating may be that university students, an elitist group by any standards, simply give in to intense pressure. Another possible reason is the philosophy of the educational system itself, which encourages learning through imitation. The whole plagiarism episode was probably more troublesome for me than for the student, since I had to strain to come to grips with what had happened in a cultural context new to me. Even now, as I write this, I am uneasy for fear that the incident will be blown completely out of proportion when, for me, it represented the opportunity to get across a lesson subtly and, I like to think, effectively. Later Chinese friends told me that the classroom indiscretion I experienced was considered minor but that cheating on a final exam or an entrance exam was serious and would bring serious punishment.

As soon as the fall semester ended, the twenty-one Fulbrighters scattered throughout China met in the southern garden city of Kunming to review our experiences and to discuss plans for the remainder of our stay. The meeting took place in late January, just after the student demonstrations and at the start of what came to be termed the backlash. There was much to talk about. In attendance were officials of the Chinese State Education Commission and U.S. Embassy officials, including Ambassador Winston Lord. Ambassador Lord, with degrees from Yale and the Fletcher School of Law and Diplomacy, has been a "China hand" for nearly two decades and U.S. ambassador to China since 1985. He is articulate, straightforward, and congenial.

At a long conference table in the *Cuihu* (Green Lake) Guest House across from peaceful Green Lake, Ambassador Lord spoke about United States–China relations. He characterized the relations as constantly wavering between "romance and hostility." The Chinese government's reaction to the student demonstrations, especially the mounting attack on bourgeois liberalism, he said, "raises questions in the United States." He acknowledged that continuity of development is important in China and added that he was optimistic about the future of United States–China relations "but not complacent."

Fulbright colleagues reported their relationships with students had been affected by the government's crackdown following student demonstrations. Students had become reluctant to visit homes of foreign faculty members. Some students seemed less eager to speak out in class. I had not had similar experiences in the classroom, at least not yet.

Outside the classroom, though, I had detected growing uneasiness and suspicion. A Chinese friend, a member of the foreign experts office staff at the Friendship Hotel, telephoned nervously one day and asked not to be quoted in any articles. He was aware that I was doing some writing while in China. In an informal conversation, we had talked about reasons for the student unrest. Nothing came up that I did not already know, but he wanted to be sure he was not identified with any part of anything I might write. This was at about the same time he and his colleagues, normally attired casually, suddenly began wearing their gray Mao jackets and buttoning them all the way up to the neck. At another institution, the Foreign Affairs College in Beijing, an American professor said his administration had instructed him to revise a final examination that had included several questions about the student demonstrations.

Meeting with us in Kunming was an official of the Chinese State Education Commission, Li Zhi Bao. He downplayed the importance of the student demonstrations and said the results would not have much impact. He added that the Chinese leadership would "stick to two positions": adherence to the four cardinal principles—the socialist road, the people's democratic dictatorship, the leadership of the Communist party, and Marxism-Leninism-Mao Zedong thought—and continuation of the open-door policy to promote national economic development. He left no doubt that China had "benefited from the open-door policy and thus will continue it."

These themes were to be repeated by other officials at the start of the spring semester. At a meeting in Beijing with the U.S. secretary of state, George Shultz, Deng Xiaoping was quoted by the *China Daily* as saying, "Why should we change the policies and principles that have been carried out and proven effective over past years? We are not going to start a campaign."

Still, many of us foreigners were anxious. My Chinese colleagues joked privately about what they called "a no-movement movement." The confusion among the Chinese, let alone among Westerners, was symptomatic of the contradictions prevailing in a society freeing itself from feudalism and moving toward the twenty-first century. But then what is a contradiction? A propositional inconsistency? Something that does not logically follow something else? Is the notion of contradiction itself dependent upon cultural context? Would a person with a Western frame of mind identify a contradiction in the same way a person with an Asian frame of mind would? Before going to China, I probably would have answered the question in the affirmative. Now, pushed to a decision, I would answer in the negative.

A Fulbright colleague, Sharon Hom, a law professor at City University of New York at Queens College, helped focus the issue for me. She is of Chinese descent and was teaching at the University of Politics and Law in Beijing. At the meeting in Kunming, she made a point that should have been obvious to us all: "We, as American experts," she said, "contribute to the contradictions inherent in China today."

The meaning of that simple statement did not register until the start of the spring semester. Suddenly there I was in front of the class, a tried-and-convicted bourgeois liberal. There was no place to hide. How do you resolve the internal contradiction of being an educator dedicated to expanding human minds while acutely aware that some things you stand for are off-limits? And what things?

I seemed to be getting a lesson in what the Chinese call a "struggle session"—coming to grips with a perplexing situation. There may have been one difference—the Chinese have "advisers" who help individuals work out a resolution acceptable to the community or work unit; I was on my own.

Part of the struggle was over the meaning of the term *bourgeois liberal*. Generally, it seemed to mean Western-style capitalism and politics, but it could be expanded conveniently to include such social issues as drugs, alcohol, homosexuality, murder, divorce, AIDS, and whatever. One definition given to us by an official of the Propaganda Ministry was "that which is opposed to the four cardinal principles." He elaborated. It meant a negation of the socialist system and "taking the capitalist road." He continued to elaborate. "It is a political concept and a political principle." He finally said it was a vague term and pleaded, "We would welcome any suggestions (for a new term) from the foreign experts." The more the elaboration, the more the confusion.

Some of the confusion, I'm sure, arose from problems of language. I knew enough about the Chinese language to be aware that translation was not an adequate term to describe converting Chinese to English and vice versa. The conversion process involves interpretation in a literal sense, that is, internalizing meaning from one frame of reference and articulating the meaning into another frame of reference. But even this cultural dimension in the interpretation of language was not the entire explanation for the confusion over the meaning of bourgeois liberalism. Political ideology was a critical element.

Such were the issues I was grappling with when Raija and I returned to Beijing. The spring semester began on a cold Monday morning. By taxi I made my way to the institute, eager to assess the mood of the class. The first discovery was that classes had been canceled for the day. There was no explanation, which in itself was not surprising, for our class schedule could be capricious. Then I was told there would be no class the rest of the week. Hmm. Maybe something more serious was going on than I had anticipated. But no. The next day a student called me at home and said the Wednesday's class had been reinstated. The on-again, off-again class meetings remained unexplained and did nothing to relieve my anxieties.

After the first several class meetings, I felt students were hesitating to speak up. They seemed to be holding back. A tension had crept into the classroom. Or was it my imagination? I decided to address what was taking place in the classroom openly and directly. I told students that despite any anxieties or social and political pressures, I could only conduct the class in the way I thought most appropriate to the continuing growth of their talents and intellects. A teacher, after all, as I reminded myself, can only teach what a teacher knows. Several students chuckled. This uncomfortable situation apparently was not new to them. We talked about goals for the semester. One student said, "We ought to do more of what we were doing last semester." After a short discussion, the entire class agreed that we should continue along the same road we had traveled the first semester. Who was teaching whom here?

Therefore, we would continue our emphasis on carrying out reporting assignments as completely, accurately, and fairly as possible. Students would continue to have access to my library, including such works as John Stuart Mill's *On Liberty,* Walter Lippmann's *Public Opinion,* and Carl Becker's *The Declaration of Independence, a Study in the History of Political Ideas.*

The realization that you are a "bourgeois liberal" and that you are contributing to contradictions is sobering, especially after growing up in the United States, where politics is regarded in terms of two-party systems and not ideologies. Thus, while contributing to what seemed like a contradiction, I came to believe that the Chinese themselves must choose what is most appropriate to their own notions of national stability and progress. It is presumptuous of us—and, for that matter, other nations—to tell them what to do.

Meanwhile, fallout from the student demonstrations would continue throughout the remainder of my stay and beyond. Not only the lives of students would be affected. In a few months, the classroom atmosphere itself would feel the effects.

16   CITIZEN STUDENTS

For months Liu Yi (not his real name) visited me regularly at the Friendship Hotel. He wanted to practice his already excellent English and was eager to help with a research project I was carrying out. He had an M.A. degree from a Chinese institution. His written facility with English was superb, and he worked on the international staff of a large organization in Beijing. He had a sharp mind and a quick grasp of ideas, and found his regular job boring, even stifling. He had set his goal — studying for a Ph.D. in the United States. He was in search of a rare commodity in China — opportunity.

In a land abundant with people, China simply does not have enough opportunity to go around. Since the late 1970s, slowly, painstakingly, opportunity has on occasion broken through a crust of rigidity and conformity. Open markets have helped create opportunities for many people, especially in the rural areas. An open-door policy toward other nations, including joint business ventures, has spawned additional opportunities. But the sector of Chinese society that suffers most from this opportunity shortage is education. Opportunities for Chinese students to study abroad or to develop their skills and intellectual gifts at home are extremely limited.

My encounter with Liu Yi was typical. Young Chinese men and women, literally thousands, eagerly pursue even the slightest sliver of hope that might lead to study abroad. Most believe that an advanced degree will create still other opportunities and rescue them from a job market that is oversupplied, heavily bureaucratized, unchallenging, and often unrewarding. Foreign experts, especially those who are teachers, quickly become targets of Chinese students seeking to realize their dreams of studying abroad.

Liu Yi, thwarted at home, had come to me to help him expand

117

his search for opportunity. If he already had been in the States, he would have had little difficulty gaining admission to any number of prestigious institutions. The intellectual promise was readily evident. The opportunity was not. Nor was the money.

During the year in China, I spent part of nearly every day informally counseling young men and women and, occasionally, middle-aged people who wanted to enter an American university or college. Chance meetings at train stations or on buses would suddenly blossom into counseling sessions on study abroad. I could have provided enough excellent students for a complete graduate program at any university in the United States.

This lack of educational opportunity is a national tragedy. It is sad to see so few chosen to study abroad from among so many who are qualified. It is also sad to see the Chinese university system itself unable to provide sufficient opportunity for young men and women to use their talents. And it is sad that many of those who study abroad do not want to return, thus depriving the country at a critical time in its development of those individuals who might be able to contribute most.

The crackdown on students following the demonstrations illustrated dramatically to me that the issue of opportunity came down to a basic social premise about the relationship of people to society. Which takes precedence? The individual or society? The Western bias is toward the individual. In China, society comes first.

In reality, and despite ideology, an individual cannot be considered separate from a society. Nor can societies be considered separate from individuals. One of the appealing attributes of my students was their desire to contribute to the building of their nation. For example, Chang Weimin, the oldest student in the class, wanted to help promote reforms in his hometown of Yinchuan in Ningxia Hui Autonomous Region. The region is one of the poorest in China. As a journalist, he felt he could assist in the move toward modernization. His attitude and that of many of his classmates bordered on the inspirational.

When it came to studying abroad, the main obstacle was usually money. Sometimes it was language. Students also had a problem obtaining sufficient foreign currency to pay for tests — such as the Graduate Record Examination and the Test of English as a Foreign Language — which are required by many American institutions. One sure place to obtain foreign currency was on the black market, but that was illegal as well as expensive. Once a student was admitted to a program abroad and managed to obtain sufficient funding, the battle had merely begun. Permission from the work unit was necessary. Several people told me that students who promised to remit part of the money from a scholarship or assistantship to their work units might stand a better chance of getting work unit approval. I did not verify any such cases, but such kickbacks seemed likely since they would bring in coveted foreign currency.

Students then had to get a passport from the Chinese government and then a visa from the country where they planned to study. Visa personnel looked for documentation of admission, evidence of sufficient financial support, and indication that the person would return to China following studies. A familiar sight outside the American Embassy office that processed visas was a line of people. They were playing the opportunity game, and the odds were about the same as the odds of a national lotto game. There were some stories of success but many of disappointment and frustration.

While it was a supreme challenge to surmount obstacles to study abroad, it may actually have been easier than being a university student in China. Though reforms have been taking place in the educational system and more are promised, changes have been slow and erratic. The nation simply has not been able to pick up the pieces left by the Cultural Revolution. During about a fifteen-year period encompassing the Cultural Revolution, no bachelor's, master's, or doctoral degrees were awarded in China. Not one! A government booklet titled "Student Unrest: What Is It All About?"—published after the 1986–1987 student demonstration—asserted pointedly that the Cultural Revolution "actually dragged China's higher education back dozens of years and planted a timebomb which exploded in later years as a serious dearth of specialized personnel."

In China the academic year ends in the summer heat of mid-July. Academically, spring is nothing special, nor is it usually very memorable except for the celebration of Spring Festival, or the Chinese Lunar New Year. This spring, however, was different. While their American counterparts were observing the traditional rites of commencement, Chinese students saw a beginning of another sort in the spring of 1987. The government's bill for the student disruptions had come due. Reforms were announced that would leave an imprint on the nation's already-troubled educational system and threaten the progress that had been achieved. By Western standards, the "reforms" were a serious step backward. To the Chinese leadership, the same reforms represented logical steps in assuring that the educational system would continue to contribute to the modernization and overall development of the country. The changes, announced and elaborated by the mass media almost daily, cut across the educational spectrum. Several areas were particularly significant and illustrated what was happening: ideology would be more important than academic work, work outside the classroom would be required before and during university studies, and regulations for studying abroad would be tightened even more.

The basis for the changes was summarized by Li Peng, then vice-premier and minister of the State Education Commission (in 1988 he became premier of the State Council). Li's report was carried by the *China Daily* (May 4, 1987): "A school should not be judged just by how many of its students enter colleges and how many postgraduates it trains. The basic criterion is whether the graduates are useful citizens, who can contribute to the socialist development of the country."

Ideology was where the severest crackdown occurred. New regulations affected students throughout their educational careers, from admission to graduation. In late April, Xinhua reported (April 29, 1987) that in admitting new students to colleges and universities in 1988, "special attention should be paid to the political, ideological and moral qualities of the candidates."

The report said admission would be denied to anyone who opposes the four cardinal principles and "refuses to mend his ways after repeated education, who commits criminal offences [*sic*] or who is morally degenerate." That meant that students who scored the highest marks would not necessarily be among the 587,000 admitted to colleges and universities.

Said education minister Li: "Last year's student demonstrations resulted from years of vague attitudes towards bourgeois liberalization. They were wrong and produced bad social effects, no matter what motives the students involved had."

Another ideological twist involved the cadres, that is, government officials or employees who are responsible for proper political and ideological education of students. They were given regular faculty rank with titles ranging from lecturers to professors. By December 1987, some cadres had been appointed to the faculty, including two at the prestigious universities of Beijing and Fudan in Shanghai. The plan called for one instructor of ideological and political thought for every 150 students. They were to carry out their political education in a variety of ways, including discussion groups.

From Hong Kong, the *South China Morning Post* (May 20, 1987) condemned the move, accusing Chinese leaders of being afraid of innovation. "Giving academic titles to party hacks," the newspaper editorialized, "is a retrograde step which all friends of China must deplore."

There was more. In late May 1988, the government announced the establishment of a Youth Ideological Education Research Center. Under the joint guidance of the Propaganda Department of the Communist Party Central Committee and the Central Committee of the Communist Youth League, the center, according to the *China Daily,* would "focus its efforts on the study of ideological and educational work among students."

Working outside of the classroom was another requirement in the wave of educational reforms. This was nothing new. During the socialist education campaign of the mid-1960s and the subsequent Cultural Revolution, students as well as faculty were sent to work in rural areas and factories. The practice was discontinued in 1977, by which time China's educational system was a shambles. Among reasons for sending students and faculty to the countryside was the feeling that students concentrating on academic work had become pampered and would not experience the real China.

The booklet "Student Unrest: What Is It All About?" claimed that many students had developed a sense of superiority, had become preoccupied with studies, and did not do chores or show concern for social affairs. Even at Beijing University, the booklet noted, one-third of the new students' parents came to the campus to help their youngsters register and to make beds for them. "In today's universities," continued the booklet, "a considerable number of students are tall but thin, because intellectual development is stressed, body-building neglected."

A vice-minister of the State Education Commission, He Dong-chang, offered a summary: "[W]hile we corrected the wrongs done by the Gang of Four [leaders of the Cultural Revolution], we have neglected the education that encourages students to do labor and keep in contact with reality."

Graduate students also felt the sting. For example, students at Qinghua University, called the MIT of China, reportedly would be required to carry out master's and doctoral research designed to solve problems in the development sector. One faculty member who had studied in the United States said—confidentially—that this policy was shortsighted since significant research in the physical sciences usually takes place in laboratories where theoretical propositions rather than practical problems guide inquiry. American universities, of course, face similar pressures; there are those who expect education to lead economic development efforts, while others maintain that the university's primary mission is to pursue knowledge.

Meanwhile, students dreaming of studying abroad now faced new regulations. Education officials asserted that sending students abroad would continue to be encouraged but that these students must study subjects suited to the needs of the country's development. Organizations in China that sponsored students abroad would select students' majors on the basis of the organization's particular needs. Students who received scholarships and stipends from foreign sources would have to obtain approval from their employers, who also had the right to demand that prospective students change majors. Students who had financial support from relatives were allowed to study in areas of their choice.

One problem with sending students abroad for study has been getting them to return. Since 1978 China has sent to more than seventy countries a total of sixty-four thousand students. To date, only about one in three has returned to China. The reasons are varied. Once abroad, many students prolong their studies. Also, expectations of work units can be unrealistic, for example, presuming a student can complete doctoral work in one or two years. Some do not return because they see limited opportunity for using their education. It is simply not known how many have decided not to return. New regulations continue to make it tougher for those who do not return. The regulations require that those who gain admission abroad must sign legally binding contracts that they will return at a specified time. In addition, relatives must vouch for the person's return.

Given these confusing and constraining educational policies, I gained a great deal of respect for the young men and women who, despite living six to eight in a dormitory room, hampered by poor libraries, separated from families, working toward an uncertain future, managed to survive and learn in the Chinese academic environment. I also admired those who successfully negotiated within the system to go abroad to study. Maybe, after all, opportunity is merely a manifestation of the individual will.

As for Liu Yi, what happened to his bid to study abroad? He began making progress. He was admitted to several institutions in the United States, but they did not provide the necessary financial support. He needed a substantial scholarship or a graduate student assistantship. As if by some miracle, that too came. A major university in New York State promised him not only an assistantship but a fellowship. He was to report in January to begin studies. But that posed another obstacle. His work unit would not permit him to leave in January. A cherished opportunity seemed on the verge of slipping away. Liu Yi wondered if the university would postpone his support and his admission to the following fall semester. He needed to know immediately. He placed a long distance telephone call to university officials and succeeded only in talking to two secretaries who could not help him. The call cost him a month's wages.

Up to this point, Liu Yi's experience was fairly typical. The ending was not: the university notified him that his admission and financial support would be held until the fall. Liu Yi is now pursuing a doctoral degree at the university.

When the United States and China officially began talking to one another fifteen years ago, one of my students was six years old; another, nineteen. Most were from nine to thirteen. One was a flower girl at an official reception for President Richard Nixon. How do these young people view relations between the two countries today? In what ways, if at all, have their views changed during the past fifteen years?

As a class assignment in the spring, I asked students to write a commentary. I gave them the choice of several topics, including how the past fifteen years of growing relations between China and the United States had affected their own lives and views. Most chose to write on this topic. The assignment came at a time when the two nations were exchanging high-level diplomatic visits, including trips to China by the secretary of defense, Caspar Weinberger, and the secretary of state, George Shultz. The student demonstrations of 1986–1987 were several months behind us, but as this assignment was about to show, the repercussions were continuing.

Students completed their articles and gave them to me. I made my usual critique and was impressed by their thoughtfulness as well as by their vivid writing style. Most students preferred writing in this subjective manner as compared to straight journalistic writing, which strives toward objectivity without, of course, ever completely achieving it. Just before class one day I found a note on my desk requesting that I see one of the officials at the institute. I discovered that this assignment had come to the attention of school authorities. They told me that from now on any student articles submitted for publication abroad must be approved beforehand. The reason was unclear. Apparently such articles might be embarrassing, although I was not sure for whom.

This restriction surprised me because I had no plans to submit any of the articles to newspapers or magazines in the States. I had told students that if any work met publication standards I might try to place the articles for them. Earlier, one student had written a side-bar—that is, a related story—for an article I had written for the *Cedar Rapids* (Iowa) *Gazette*. Also I had written a piece based on information provided by students that appeared in a U.S. national journalism trade publication. I received $150 for the article and gave it to the class. I never did find out if the students got the money. It may have gone to the institute or to the students' work units.

After this assignment and in the wake of mounting attacks on "bourgeois liberalism," students also had become aware of the authorities' interest in their work. They were concerned. After all, their careers were at stake. I was not about to do anything that might jeopardize those careers. So I thought it best to keep the papers in my possession. After returning the papers to the students so they could get my assessment, I collected them and promised the students that I would not show the articles to anyone.

At one point, I considered destroying the articles. For reasons I cannot recall, I kept them. In fact, I had forgotten about them until months after I left China and they showed up in a crate of personal possessions Raija and I had shipped by boat from China. I reread the students' work and was even more impressed than before.

Their comments are illuminating for several reasons. They show how much the attitudes of Chinese people have changed toward the United States, how American teachers often represented turning points in students' perceptions of the United States, and how the students' attitudes about America were shaped by their government through mass media and parents. They also reveal the practical political side of renewing relations with the United States in light of China's Russian relations, which at the time were deteriorating. Most importantly, however, I think the students' papers illustrate dramatically how perceptions of people toward people of another country can change drastically over a relatively brief period of time. I have maintained confidentiality of authorship.

One student, born in the late 1950s, wrote:

> The country USA first hit my little head in a Chinese feature film named *The Heroic Sons and Daughters*. Depicting the early 1950s Korean War, the film recorded a heavy battle between the Chinese people's volunteers and American troops. A scene showed

bloody bayonet fighting, leaving an unforgettable memory in my mind.

"What do the words 'USA' and symbol of the skull on the enemy's helmets mean?" I asked my mother. "They are Yankees and great killers," my mother told me. At that time I was 10 years old and knew the USA was a terrible devil.

In the following years American imperialists filled China's newspapers and radio broadcasts. A cartoon showing an American soldier trapped in a pit with pointed bamboo-shoots and films of American bombers shelling the cities and villages of Vietnam are still fresh to me even today.

At that time I didn't know why the United States, a country on another side of the globe, came so far to fight against our neighbors. Thus, the mixed feeling of hatred and dread had been nurtured in my heart and kept growing until the year 1972 when China shook hands with its former Number 1 enemy through signing the Shanghai Communiqué.

Another student, age fourteen at the time of Nixon's visit, echoed similar sentiments:

> The first American I became familiar with was President Lyndon Johnson nicknamed "meiguolao" (Chinese for "yankee") and cartooned on walls and in newspapers during the Vietnam War. The image was ugly and notorious. Wearing a long cap and with a big nose, Johnson held a long sword in his hand, blood dripping at the tip.
>
> From then on "Yankee" became a symbol of hostility and cruelty in China. The term, therefore, was often used to refer to "bad eggs" in children's games, or to label a mischievous child.

Another student was nine years old and in primary school when Nixon arrived in China:

> I only knew that Nixon was the head of the helmeted, carbine-holding American GIs I saw in films depicting Vietnam and Korean wars.
>
> At that time, our [primary school] teacher often asked us to notice the slogans at the airport: "Don't you see that we only write: 'To Receive US President Richard Nixon' rather than 'warmly welcome,' which we use for leaders of North Korea and Albania? To normalize relations with the United States is only to make use of it."

Another student, eight years old at the time of President Nixon's visit, remembers struggling atop a stool to locate the United States on a wall map. He was unsuccessful and finally penciled in a piece of

land east of Taiwan to stand for the nation that was more friendly
toward the Chinese island community than the Chinese mainland.

> My knowledge of the United States was so limited that, when it
> was mentioned, I could think of nothing but a bandage-bound tiger,
> struggling in a trap called Vietnam and stabbed by thousands of
> bamboo spears.
>
> In early 1972, upon hearing the sudden news that then U.S.
> President Richard Nixon was visiting China and talking with
> Chinese leaders, I asked myself: "Would there be any danger for our
> Great Leader Chairman Mao when meeting with such a bad man?"

Later, the same student wrote, he counted himself among the benefi-
ciaries of the diplomatic breakthrough.

Another student wrote of the inner conflict in trying to understand what was taking place between the United States and China:

> I still remember my impression of the United States as a child
> was that of an imperial country. Mass media of our country at that
> time presented an image of it as a monster, killing Chinese people,
> looting and pillaging China's resources.
>
> So when John Kennedy, then U.S. President, was assassinated
> in 1963, I, as well as many others of my age, hailed his death. I knew
> nothing about what on earth he had done. I only hated him because
> he was the number one man in that damned country.
>
> I hoped so eagerly to grow up and join the army so that I could
> have the opportunity to fight U.S. GIs like the heroes I saw in books
> and movies.
>
> Word came in 1972 that China and the United States had signed
> a Shanghai Communiqué. Both countries were about to become
> friends.
>
> I was working in a machine tool factory then. It was difficult to
> understand why we should [become friends].
>
> Not until five years later did my view of the United States begin
> to change when I began studying English [at a university].

Another student wrote about his change of attitude:

> In my mind, "imperialist" gave way to "diversity"; "devil" dis-
> appeared while "humanism" came in. The sun was found to shine
> not only in the Orient but in the Western world as well. Christopher
> Columbus discovered America geographically in 1492 and nearly
> 500 years later some Chinese, especially the young, seemed to have
> refound the continent as a cultural treasury.

Another student reflected a pragmatic view of the politics of the

Asia-Pacific region. He argued in his commentary that the Chinese were looking for a force to repel Soviet pressure, while the United States was interested in a unified China to counteract the possibility of Soviet expansion in the region.

> In other words, Sino-U.S. relations boil down to a natural product born to meet the needs of the international situation rather than those of the goodwill of both people.
>
> To be sure, with the expansion of the Soviet interest in the Asia-Pacific region, Beijing and Washington will embrace each other ever closer. Bilateral relations will further improve. Both sides will benefit from each other even more.
>
> But in between is an engine fueled with gasoline refined out of the essential conflict between communism and capitalism. Handshakes can only be viewed as an expedient measure although it could last for a considerably long time into the future.

The shift in the students' attitudes toward America and Americans occurred dramatically. For most, the change came in a personal way: exposure to an American teaching in China.

> It is in the university where for the first time I came across Americans. They taught English and American literature. From their lectures and my personal contacts with them, I found they were in general kind and polite, and most of them had a sense of humor. Thus, my abstract impression of the States turned into a concrete picture.

Wrote another:

> Immediately after Nixon's visit, students in my school started learning English as their foreign language instead of Russian. Ever since then, the magic language has accompanied me and motivated my life.

For the first time this generation of Chinese began encountering American history and culture:

> I was eager to join the army of English learners. Through efforts I enrolled in a night school, where I attended courses in English and Chinese literature. A window was opened in my mind thereafter.

Through the window entered American history—the Revolution, the Civil War, the Great Depression, the civil rights movement, and women's liberation. Benjamin Franklin and Thomas Jefferson. Mark Twain and Ernest Hemingway. Coca-Cola and *Love Story.* Abraham

Lincoln, Franklin D. Roosevelt, and John F. Kennedy.

Not all experiences with American teachers were positive. One student, who earlier had grown fond of an American English-language teacher, wrote about another teacher from the States he had encountered. It may have been a classic case of culture clash:

> When my classmates asked if he [the teacher] could be kind with them, his answer was: "As a teacher, if students think I'm kind, there must be something wrong with me."
>
> Even private conversation with him was difficult because of his embarrassing questions and remarks. I still remember one of his poetic sentences spoken in front of our classroom building: "Look at your buildings, Mr. [the student's name]. They are all gray. No liberty. No freedom." Such remarks made most of my classmates, even department leaders, think he might be an FBI [the student here apparently meant CIA] agent. Later it was said that he once fought in Korea as a squad leader.

One student who had worked as a tourist guide for China Travel Service recalled a poignant personal encounter on a scenic boat trip she had made with Americans from Guilin to Yangshuo on the Li River in southern China:

> The man looked insatiable in enjoying the beauty of the river and the flanked mountains, using a pair of binoculars from time to time. Then he told me he had suffered poor eyesight for years and received several operations on his eyes. Earlier his doctor warned him he could lose his eyesight completely in a few months, which prompted him on the tour to China.
>
> I was tearful when he said, "I want to keep these beautiful pictures in my mind so that I can recall them after I am blind."

Another student, who had failed the examination for the institute twice before passing it, wrote eloquently about how he had been influenced by what he had learned about American history and culture through television, movies, and books:

> Through these channels I have more and better understanding of the Americans who are also human beings of flesh and blood like ourselves. I don't think it deniable that there exists a kind of mist in parts of the world or over the whole world, mist that muffles people's eyes and gives a distorted vision of the world. I can't tell who or what is to blame. But at least it seems to me, if there were less misunderstanding and distorted impressions, history would be marked with fewer mistakes.

A teacher can learn a lot from students.

18 SAPLINGS

Fifteen-year-old Wang Jan Hua appeared to be waiting for me as I dismounted my bike, parked it, and began the trek by foot up Moon Hill. I had gone nearly an hour out of Yangshuo in south China past water buffaloes and rice fields and through what may be the most beautiful landscape in China. On this chilly and overcast Sunday morning in April, Wang Jan Hua had made a catch.

"You are my English lesson," he proclaimed.

"You are my guide," I told him.

"I like English," said the friendly youngster.

"Do you study English in school?" I asked, making my way up the steep path toward a limestone peak with a moon-shaped hole through it.

"Yes, every . . . I mean, each day, I study English. Teacher . . . my teacher tells . . . told me to study. Not school . . . on days no school, I should study too."

Along the path he pointed to trees and told me he and his classmates had planted them.

"This mine," he said proudly.

Remembering a photo I had seen a month or so earlier of Chinese officials planting trees around Beijing, I asked if he knew that Deng Xiaoping encouraged the planting of trees.

He replied that this was why the trees had been planted, adding, "Deng Xiaoping very good. Deng Xiaoping very good."

"Do you know the word for a young tree?" I asked.

"No."

"Sapling," I said. "A sapling is a young tree."

"Sap . . ., sap . . .," he struggled.

130

"Ling," I interceded. "Sap-ling."

"Sap . . . , sap. . . ." He concentrated, then exploded, "Sap-ling."

"Henhao," I exclaimed, showing off my limited Chinese vocabulary. The phrase means very good or excellent.

And that was how our hour went. I did not try to explain that young people also can be referred to as saplings. But the image of saplings growing and developing together remains vivid in my mind.

For a visitor to China, especially the China off the beaten path, the experience is nothing unusual. The Chinese, along with many other Asians, are eager to learn English. Their zeal is remarkable. In fact, if you're interested in practicing your Chinese, the opportunities are limited. Everyone there wants to practice English.

"How old are you?" was the first question put by a bicyclist who had passed me as I was biking on a Beijing street. He had noticed I was a *waiguoren* (foreigner) and had slowed down. Here was a chance for him to practice English. The age question is among the first visitors are asked in China. Newcomers may think the question is rude, but in China it is not. Traditionally, respect and age increase together. I enjoyed growing older in China.

Our conversation continued through intersections and around other cyclists. After finding out what I was doing in Beijing, my cycling companion had another standard question: "How much do you get paid?"

I came to regard such questions not as invasions of privacy but merely as opportunities for persons to practice their English, and I tried to be responsive. On the salary question, though, I was usually vague; somehow my culture told me that was too private.

For my students, English was not a problem, and all instruction was in English. Most will travel abroad, and some may become correspondents in English-speaking countries. Nearly all had majored in English as undergraduates, and many had worked as interpreters. They were every bit as competent in the mechanics of language as are university students in America. But sometimes dictionary definitions could be taken too literally.

During one class, the topic of women's liberation came up in an interview with a journalist couple from California. The woman talked about how she and her husband were doing the same job in China but that she got paid considerably less. The same thing happened in the United States, she told the students. Not only that, but women have responsibility for the children. In a story based on this interview, a student wrote that in America "women have to work all day and then go home and breed."

Later a friend told me about the magazine reporter doing a story about the growth of free enterprise in the Chinese economic system. He wrote about a merchant who reaped great profits from "selling concubines." Although probably potentially profitable, this particular enterprise did not seem correct given the context. The merchant, it turned out, was a vegetable vendor and was getting rich selling cucumbers.

Translating to or from Chinese, I discovered, is not easy. I developed great respect for those who are proficient at it. Americans have not been strong in foreign languages. Translation from or to Chinese does not depend on seeking equivalent word-for-word or phrase-for-phrase meanings. Chinese calls for understanding—fully comprehending—the meaning and then re-expressing it in the other language. In such a complex enterprise, strange and sometimes humorous things happen.

A sign for hair styling appeared at a doorway of a building along Beiheyan, a short street not far from the Forbidden City. I stopped my bike and recorded the message as faithfully as I could:

SMALL GOL-
DFISH LADY H-
AIR DRESSING
HOUSE SPECIA-
LIST IN DIFFE-
RENT DOMESTIC
AND FOREIGN
LADY HADY DRE-
SSING STYLE

Names of dishes on the menu at our Friendship Hotel dining hall, which regularly served both Chinese and Western meals as well as dishes from other parts of the world, conveyed their own gustatory charm: "Strange flavour beef," "Stir-fried malabar nightshade and bamboo," "Stir-fried three kinds," "Two kinds in sauce," and "Three corners with spinach." The names were usually more exotic than the tastes.

One day, while browsing on the first floor of Beijing's largest department store, appropriately called No. 1 Department Store, I spied a three-by-five-foot sign in the cosmetics section advertising a body cream called Venus. Here it is as it appeared in agonized English and tortured spellings:

> Very often, the small breasts which have not outgrown in the childhood stage "Jiah Ru Ling" breast cream will quickly corret this defect.
>
> The breasts which are dropping or flacid, it happens after breast-feeding, there it will restore breasts to their normolly size.

The advertisement did not fare well during the campaign against "bourgeois liberalism." It soon came down.

At an art gallery in Lhasa, Tibet, customers were assured that any purchases would receive careful handling. A sign on a wall said:

> For your big painting you bought
> We are going to put a stick inside
> and will roll and wrap it carefully.
> Your painting will be safe from our experience.

A person could get the message. And isn't that what counts?

Millions of Chinese seek to improve their English by tuning in to the Voice of America and the BBC. The VOA reports an audience of twenty million in China. In several cities, "English Corners" are also popular. These are places, usually in parks, where people come to practice speaking English. English-speaking foreigners are especially welcome.

In Beijing, there was a gathering in the English Corner every Sunday morning in Purple Bamboo Park just across from the Capital Gymnasium. Mostly, Chinese university students took part. The corner was set up in 1984 for the express purpose of providing practice for those studying English by correspondence.

On a fall Sunday in 1986, amid the trees, playgrounds, and the lake, several hundred persons had gathered. A British and American couple strolled into the park and were immediately engulfed.

"What do American students think of Chinese students who go to the United States to study?"

"How do students in America live? Do they have to get jobs to pay for tuition? What do people in America know about Marxism?"

Sometimes the questions could not be understood the first time around. Often they could not be answered to the satisfaction of the participants.

"What do you think about terrorism in Europe?"

"What do you think about Chinese philosophy?"

The questions were endless. Answers varied by respondent and quickly gave way to exhaustion.

Sometimes efforts to help others backfired. This happened in the case of a young man who befriended me at the main office of the Civil Aviation Administration of China (CAAC) in Beijing. I had gone to the window for non-Chinese travelers to purchase tickets for a trip to Shanghai. With some difficulty, a woman clerk was trying to help me. Then another clerk, a pleasant, smiling fellow with a good command of English, intervened and asked, "May I help you?"

We struck up a conversation, and after making the reservations, we continued talking in a hallway adjacent to the window.

"I like Iacocca," Zhang (not his real name) told me, referring to the Chrysler Company president, Lee Iacocca.

"Many people like him," I responded.

"I'd like to be like him," he went on.

"Your English is quite good," I said. "How did you learn your English?"

"I study myself. I have no chance to go to university," Zhang said. "The Cultural Revolution," he explained.

A few weeks passed. I returned to pick up the tickets to Shanghai.

Zhang gave me the tickets. Impressed earlier when he told me he had learned English on his own, I decided to help him. I presented him with two small textbooks. The books were printed in English on one page with the same text in Chinese on the facing page. He was grateful.

A few months later he telephoned and asked if he could see me. I told him, of course. One evening about 10 p.m., after he got off work, he came to the hotel.

He was in trouble, he told me. His colleagues had seen me give him the books and had reported him. His supervisor, he told me, had confiscated the books. Further, his monthly bonus for November had been withheld. Could I help? I felt miserable and was not sure there was anything I could do, but I told him I would try.

About a month later, with an interpreter, I went to the CAAC office and searched out Mr. Zhang's supervisor. Clad nattily in a blue suit, he was seated at a computer terminal. I extended a name card, which identified me in both Chinese and English. He refused to take it. My interpreter tried to explain the situation, that I meant no harm with the books and intended only to help. The supervisor, avoiding my gaze, said matter-of-factly that Mr. Zhang had other problems too.

Perhaps the main problem, my interpreter friend and I surmised later, was that Mr. Zhang was ambitious and resourceful and his co-workers did not like that.

A week or so later, Mr. Zhang telephoned to thank me for trying to help him.

"Has anything changed?" I asked.

"No."

19   THREE "SEES"

Living an extended period of time in Beijing permits the luxury of exploring sites on one's own terms. Visitors traveling quickly in and out get an all-too-predictable, conveyor-belt tour that sweeps them in air-conditioned buses to the Forbidden City, to the Great Wall, and to a helping of the famous Peking roast duck. Rounding out the tour might be the Summer Palace, the Temple of Heaven, a brief stop at the zoo so people can say they've seen pandas in China, and an hour at the Friendship Store to stock up on souvenirs. It is not exactly a cultural experience.

With high-rise apartments and hotels springing up like so many modern temples, and with freeways replacing the old walls of the city, Beijing has been undergoing a transformation comparable to the changes in the economic and social sectors. It does not take long to notice that the city is rife with pollution; industrial air mingling with dust from the Gobi Desert often darkens the skies and blots out the sun. Springtime is the worst. A face mask is recommended for biking, but even with a mask a person can feel the grime on the skin and the grit against the teeth. There is not much grass except what grows in the parks. And although colorful, Western-style garb is changing the drabness, the color of Beijing is basically gray, with brown prevailing in the winter.

Nonetheless, Beijing possesses such an array of sights and sounds and smells that even year-long residents have the chance to sample only a few. There are bird and cricket markets, parks throughout the city, crowded shopping areas, free markets, countless temples in various states of disrepair, tombs, specialty shops for such items as chopsticks, traditional Chinese costumes, and an herbal medicine store in the old Dazhalan area south of Tiananmen Square that dates to the

Qing dynasty (A.D. 1644–1911). A sign above the entrance to the pharmacy indicates that someone is familiar with Latin: *suppositoria haemorrhoidini.*

Raija and I especially enjoyed Beijing's safe streets, day or night. We also appreciated the accessibility of the city. A bicycle was all a person needed. We each had three special places a little off the beaten path.

For me, one such place was south of Tiananmen Square near Qianmen (Front Gate). Here in the busy Dazhalan shopping area, we were threading our way through the crowds trying to follow our guide. About the time we thought the guide had taken a wrong turn, he directed us into a clothing shop. A man behind a service counter pushed a button. Part of the floor slid away—à la James Bond— revealing concrete steps and an entrance. Welcome to Beijing Underground.

It is mole city, except that this one has human-size walkways. Some passage doors glide electrically. Others are concrete several inches thick and must be pushed manually. Claustrophobes would have a hard time here. Although now primarily a tourist attraction, underground Beijing was built to provide protection in case of war. Construction began in 1969, when relations between China and the Soviet Union were tense. The government financed construction, and millions of people, including children, contributed labor.

In the bowels of Beijing, we sat down at a long table in a meeting room for a briefing from an official. He pulled back a velvet curtain, revealing an electronic map with multicolored lights showing different parts of the labyrinth. Such technology would have been welcome in my classroom. No photos, he said, heightening the intrigue.

The statistics were impressive, although there was nothing to compare them to. It had taken ten years to complete. There are two levels, one at eight meters, another at fifteen (we were at the eight-meter level). There are forty-five underground shops employing two thousand persons. The place has its own electricity-generating plant, a department store, restaurants, warehouses, a telephone system, air filters, and about ninety entrances. The entire complex could accommodate five million persons. It was not clear what would happen to Beijing's other four million residents. Food? None for disasters, although there are several underground restaurants. One passageway leads to the city's famous Qianmen Roast Duck Restaurant. Obviously, a person would have to make reservations early.

Not far from Dazhalan, back at Tiananmen Square, was another place that attracted me for historical reasons. Four abreast, in a line snaking for several blocks, people were waiting to enter a large hall just east of the Great Hall of the People. As foreign visitors, we were allowed to cut in near the front. But first we had to check our cameras and bags. The wait to the entrance took only a few minutes. Two persons split off to the left, two to the right. Suddenly we were in the Mao Zedong Memorial Hall to see the body of the man who had profoundly influenced China and altered the lives of billions of people.

Accompanying us on this spring morning was one of my students, Zhang Xiaoquan, from Tianjin. When she discovered we planned to visit the mausoleum, she offered to accompany us as a chance to practice her English. As we moved forward, guards and loudspeakers admonished us to be respectful. Madame Zhang—we called her "madame" since she had spent some time in France—told us the crowd was not nearly as somber as it was a few years ago.

"People used to come and weep," she said. "Now they seem to come out of curiosity." This is part of the discrediting of Mao since the Cultural Revolution. "He's still a great man," Madame Zhang quickly added. "But he made mistakes."

The Chinese, who like to quantify things, now say the good-to-bad ratio on Mao is seventy to thirty, with a trend toward even more balancing of the percentages. A personality cult had grown up around him, but now the Mao statues, once plentiful throughout China, have largely disappeared (since our departure, the large statue in front of Beijing University's library has been removed). Construction of the one-hundred-foot-high mausoleum began a little more than a month after Mao died September 9, 1976. On the first anniversary of the Great Helmsman's death in 1977, the building was inaugurated.

The line of people, mostly Chinese, moved quickly. We walked past a statue of Mao and entered the mausoleum. Mao's body is draped in the red flag of China's Communist party, and only the upper part of the body is visible. The face is unmistakably Mao's. His face has a shiny, plastic look in contrast to that of another comrade, Vladimir Lenin, which—I remembered from years ago on a visit to Moscow's Red Square—had a chalky appearance.

An hour's ride by bus southwest of Beijing took us to see another celebrated member of the human species. I was interested, again, because of the place's historical significance. But first, en route, we stopped at China's most famous bridge, described by Marco Polo during a thirteenth century visit as the most beautiful he had ever

A STATUE of Chairman Mao Zedong stood in front of the library at Beijing University, where students traditionally have been in the forefront of change. This picture was taken in 1987, before the statue was toppled and removed.

seen. Originally built in 1192, the bridge features balusters decorated with nearly five hundred intricately carved stone statues of lions, each distinctive in appearance and varying in height from two feet to a few inches. For the Chinese, the Marco Polo Bridge also evokes bitter memories. It is the place where in 1937 Japanese and Chinese troops exchanged gunfire, provoking full-scale war. Looking closely, we could find pockmarks in the stone from bullets. Today, traffic over the bridge is restricted to people on foot, bikes, and horse-drawn carts.

Beyond the bridge a few more kilometers, we entered the town of Zhoukoudian, nestled in foothills and coal pits. Here is a park with an exhibit hall and a series of caves, where archaeologists have been digging since 1921. We strolled to a hill where human remains were discovered that go back twenty thousand years. Then we walked to a nearby site, descended a few steps, and saw a wooden sign bearing Chinese characters and the date 1929.

It was on a December afternoon of that year that a skull was unearthed which came to be an important link in the development of theories relating to the origin of man. The complete skullcap — Peking man (*Sinanthropus pekinensis*) — established a link to humankind that reached back about five hundred thousand years. The exhibit hall has a replica of the skull. The whereabouts of the real skull is a mystery. It was packed away when the Japanese invaded in 1937 and has never been found.

Raija had her own special places in Beijing. Nearly every day she told about new discoveries, usually markets of one sort or another, that she had made on her bike.

One such market was on West Pinganli Street in an out-of-the-way area not far from the Beijing Zoo. It was a bird and fish market, one of several around the city. The market thrived on a favorite custom of elderly men — buying and keeping birds as pets. In the morning, the old men head for parks on their bikes with bird cages hanging from handlebars or secured to the passenger seat over the rear wheel. In transit, the bird men cover the cages with cloth. In the park, the men lounge around and chatter with one another, just as the birds seem to do. It struck me as a fine way to pass the time — communing with birds, nature, and friends.

At the Pinganli market, a man with a straggly beard and mustache, wearing a blue shirt with dark vest, operated a bird stall. He sat at a table amid wire and bamboo cages, hooks for the cages, tiny dishes that are used as bird feeders, other bird paraphernalia, and a metal cash box. Another "birder" had a wire cage with green, yellow,

ELDERLY CHINESE MEN lounge in a park, their pet birds in cages hanging from tree branches.

and blue birds fluttering inside. Another sold grain and sunflower seeds. One stall offered fish. Customers, hands behind their backs, pushed up against the table and leaned forward to inspect items. Prices are always negotiable, and birds with bright and shiny feathers bring the best prices. Nearby, outdoor barbers were plying their trade.

Raija also enjoyed wandering the old alleyways in the north of town around the old Drum and Bell towers. Here were old men and women relaxing. Men tottered along on canes. Women looked after grandchildren. People sat near doorways, which led into courtyards housing perhaps a dozen families with three and four generations represented. Public restrooms added a pungent aroma. Some of the elderly women wore small black slippers over tiny misshapen feet, a result of the foot-binding custom that began a thousand years ago and lasted into the early 1900s. The practice, now prohibited, is said to have begun in court circles and spread to the upper classes. Westerners cannot comprehend such a practice, but then the tight corsets

YOUNGSTERS are taken for a stroll in Beijing.

of the eighteenth and nineteenth centuries are probably equally baffling to the Chinese.

In this north side area, situated along a lake is the former home of Madame Song Qingling (1892–1981), wife of Sun Yatsen, the nation's founder. The double-eaved mansion, once the home of Prince Zai Feng, father of China's last emperor, Pu Yi, sits in a garden as relaxing as the names of the mansion's rooms: Studio of Openmindedness, Room for Listening to the Orioles, and Room for Listening to Rain. The house was turned into a museum after Madame Song's death. Photos and other relics portray much of the history of China during the twentieth century.

In this same area is a restaurant that Raija believes serves the best food in all of China. It is a tiny place in a family's home and is called "Family Li's Dishes." It features imperial cuisine. Located among the rows of narrow alleyways at No. 11 Yang Fang Hutong, the family-

Ms. Li Li of "Family Li's Dishes"

operated restaurant does not have a sign, only a plain wooden door leading into a courtyard, where other families live. You have to make reservations, and that is not easy to do. The Li family does not have a phone. You must place a call to a nearby public phone, leave a message—in Chinese—and then wait for a return call. Even taxi drivers get lost finding the place.

The chef is twenty-eight-year-old Ms. Li Li, who works in a kitchen the size of a clothes closet. Her father and brother serve guests in a dining room that has been converted from a bedroom. One round table with a revolving tray nearly fills the room. There is seating for a dozen people, no more. The meal literally is a feast fit for emperors, since Li Li's great-grandfather worked as a steward for the court of Empress Dowager Wu Cixi in the Qing dynasty.

When we ate there, the first dish was honeyed walnuts. The last dish, the twenty-fourth course, was Peking roast duck.

20 TWO "SPENDS"

The most popular open market among visitors to Beijing is along Xiushui East Street near the Jianguomen diplomatic compound, midway between the Beijing Friendship Store and the Jianguo Hotel. The market has more than 150 small shops on either side of a lane about 50 feet wide and 500 feet long. Shoppers jostle with one another to inspect goods as vendors, men and women of all ages, sit in the stalls and eagerly negotiate prices with shoppers.

Most stalls handle clothing, though a few sell fruits and vegetables. The garments lie in stacks on tables and hang from improvised racks. There is no dressing room. If you want to try on something, you just slip it over whatever you are wearing at the time. Many items carry brand names and are manufactured in China for export throughout the world. The Chinese people like to shop here because ordinarily they do not have access to export goods in the domestic market. Many of the items, one can see upon close inspection, are "seconds" and have been rejected for export. A shopper has to be careful. A consolation is that even purchase of a flawed product is not going to cost a visitor enough to get agitated about. The market is open every day.

The market represents the dramatic economic shift by the government in the late 1980s to encourage individual enterprise. Many of the vendors are wealthy by Chinese standards. Those who have profited handsomely are known as "ten-thousand-*yuan* households," although "million-*yuan* households" also have appeared on the scene. As you walk along the stalls, vendors frequently whisper something that may not be intelligible to the inexperienced ear but to the seasoned ear is familiar: "Change money? Change money?" Thus, the market not only represents free enterprise in China but something else: an opportunity for the individual entrepreneur to exchange money illegally (in Chinese, *daohui*).

In fact, China has a thriving black market for money. Just as the Xiushui East Street Market has two faces, so does China's currency system. There is one currency called *renminbi,* shortened conversationally to the letters RMB and meaning "people's money." Then there is foreign-exchange currency. It is referred to as FEC and is often called "new money" but also "tourist money," because it is the kind of money tourists get when they enter the country and exchange dollars, marks, yen, or rupees. These two classes of money and the distinctions between them remain largely concealed to the tourist. But the person who spends an extended period of time in China will encounter the two-money system, often in unpleasant ways. It is a complex and intriguing situation. And if money talks, FEC speaks louder than RMB by 50 percent or more. If you are confused, you are not alone.

Typical was this woman, an American traveling in Guilin in south China, who stopped at a cloisonné souvenir counter at the Reed Flute Cave. She was ready to make a purchase. Waving FEC notes, she asked her husband, "How many dollars for fourteen of these?"

"I don't know," he responded and then surmised, "but I think quite a few."

The two-money system is a particularly thorny issue because government leaders are well aware of the existence of a thriving currency black market. The two currencies, however, are believed necessary for the nation to be able to attract foreign venture capital. While economic changes have spurred development and initiative, the current money system, instituted in 1980, has promoted a black market that gives the impression of capitalism running amok.

It took several months for Raija and me to understand China's currency. To begin with, it is necessary to remember those two basic types of currency: RMB and FEC. RMB and FEC notes physically resemble monopoly money, but they are real.

The basic Chinese currency unit is the *yuan.* The *yuan* is divided into *jiao* and *fen.* Ten *fen* make one *jiao,* and ten *jiao* make one *yuan.* Adding what seems to be unnecessary complication is a distinction in the use of these terms in written and spoken Chinese. When speaking, such as in counting change, Chinese refer to *yuan* as *kuai* and to *jiao* as *mao.*

FEC, the "tourist money," has denominations ranging from one to one hundred, the one-hundred-*yuan* note being the highest. For a long time, the largest RMB note was ten. Foreign experts, who received a portion of their money in RMB, sometimes told of the embarrassment of being paid with large stacks of RMB notes. Their Chinese counterparts, paid considerably less than the foreign experts, must have wondered about class distinctions. In spring 1987, the government began issuing RMB currency in fifty- and one-hundred-*yuan* denominations. This in itself suggested growing prosperity among the Chinese, but inflation and convenience were probably the main reasons for the higher denominations.

Physically, it is easy to distinguish FEC from RMB. There is the visual "wear test." FEC notes tend to be new and wrinkle free. RMB notes are usually crumpled, dirty, and well worn.

China introduced FEC in 1980 to promote the infusion of foreign currency. FEC is privileged money. With FEC, a person can buy goods imported to China, make purchases at special shops, and change back to dollars — all things that cannot be done with RMB. A person converting money to Chinese currency gets FEC. The official government rate at the time we were there was 3.7 *yuan* for $1 U.S.

The actual cost of things in China depends on who you are and what you are buying. For air tickets, as an example, Chinese pay about half of what tourists pay. Foreign experts, on the other hand, get a discount, which is about a third off of what tourists pay.

Normally tourists are required to pay for goods and services with FEC. Chinese, legally, have only RMB. Foreign experts usually have both RMB and FEC, receiving a portion of their salaries in both currencies. But foreign experts have something more important — the exalted "white card." It is just that — a nine-by-four-inch card containing each persons's passport-size photo. Folded into thirds, it is about the size of a credit card. This card says the recipient is authorized to spend RMB.

Now the plot turns seamy, some might say capitalistic.

Many Chinese covet the FEC because it buys foreign goods and can be converted into real foreign currency, like U.S. dollars. In fact, students taking foreign examinations to study abroad (such as the Test of English as a Foreign Language) must pay with foreign currency to take the exam. One way foreign currency can be obtained is through purchase on the black market with RMB. Because of the demand among the Chinese for FEC, a black market for exchanging FEC and RMB has sprung up in many parts of the country, especially in places frequented by tourists. The prevailing rate of exchange at the time we were there was 150 RMB for 100 FEC. That is a 50-percent return on investment plus points for bourgeois liberalization.

In Yangshuo, an idyllic riverside village in the south, a young Swede said he got a rate of 160 RMB for 100 FEC. That was in Guangzhou, which has a thriving black market. The reason for the high rate, he said, was volume. He exchanged 1,000 FEC.

If you walk along busy shopping areas or outside tourist hotels in Kunming, Hangzhou, Shanghai, and Beijing, the most-heard phrase you hear is "Change money? Change money?" Young and old women, children, and all sorts of men — from yuppie to sleazy — obviously regard this practice as profitable despite its being illegal. Kunming in the south probably has the most charming money changers. Women, in colorful ethnic dress, children clinging to their backs in slings, patrol entrances to hotels. They carry baskets containing handicrafts for sale and have mastered the phrase "Change money?" Actual transactions do not ordinarily occur in highly public places but along side streets, behind a wall, or in a market stall. Occasionally police mount a crackdown, but it is usually mild with a few resulting arrests mainly for show.

The hunger for FEC is so great that individuals with legitimate white cards encounter grumbling from taxi drivers and merchants when they pay in RMB. "You do it," said the holder of a white card and a year-long resident of China, "and they look at you like you're the scum of the earth."

In Shanghai I had lunch at the Youyou Restaurant in a new high-rise office building downtown. The meal was tasty. The bill was 47.3 *yuan* (equal, at the official exchange rate, to $12.78 U.S.). I happened to have some RMB and proffered the money with my white card.

The smiling hostess said, "We do not accept white cards."

I decided to see how far this could be pushed, since I was unaware that it was possible to reject such a card in this circumstance. The hostess said the restaurant would have to add 30 percent to my bill if I paid in RMB. This add-on, to make up the differential between FEC and RMB, is also a common practice.

"No," I said, "I do not think that is legally permissible."

I asked to see the manager. He or she did not want to see me. The

IN THE STONE FOREST near Kunming, women from one of China's more than fifty ethnic minority groups, the Sani, sell their handiwork.

TWO ELDERLY WOMEN relax in an open market in Kunming.

hostess shuttled messages back and forth. The restaurant finally accepted the RMB, but the hostess, still smiling, told me to bring FEC next time.

A foreign expert from Canada wrote a letter to the *China Daily* (March 10, 1987) urging government authorities to do something about the confused and illegal currency activities. He recounted an incident in the southern Chinese city of Guangzhou, formerly Canton, where he had a beer in a hotel with friends. He wanted to pay in RMB, the currency in which he was being paid in China. The manager said he could not accept RMB since the hotel was a joint venture, that is, operated jointly by foreign and Chinese firms. The foreign expert objected, and the manager finally blurted out, "This is not China."

The currency system is pernicious. It debases the official currency in favor of the foreign-exchange certificates and encourages the black market. The Chinese government, of course, is aware of the problems. For a number of years officials have said plans were under way to abolish FEC and to adopt RMB as the sole Chinese currency. But eliminating FEC would lead to other problems, particularly among foreign firms that want to be able to convert FEC to their own national currency to take money out of the country.

Meanwhile, China's two-money system thrives, creating confusion and consternation — as well as entrepreneurial opportunities.

The warm, tropical rain was beating
down, and we began regretting that
we had rented bicycles this mid-April
day. It appeared as though the damp
weather was here to stay. On a trip to south China, Raija and I had
decided to arrange the itinerary so we could visit Guilin. It is a place
where visitors think they may have been before. For this is the area
that has inspired Chinese poets and artists whose works have taught
us what China should look like.

The scenes in this part of China evoke vivid images of strange-
looking peaks draped in silky mist and tufts of clouds; barefoot
peasants, pant legs rolled up, tilling rice fields with water buffalo;
people fishing from sleek bamboo boats, ingeniously snaring their
catch using long-necked, hook-billed birds; women washing clothes
by hand along the banks of the river; junks and sampans tied on the
shoreline with clothes hanging out to dry; lush green countryside unfolding in neat terraces in all directions; and, finally, a serenity that
seems possible only when nature and people live in harmony.

Guilin is a bustling city of three hundred thousand in Guangxi
Zhuang Autonomous Region, where a mixture of different ethnic
groups live. The city is situated amidst magical mountains and is one
of China's top tourist attractions. This is where the Chinese themselves go to take in the sights.

The odd mountain peaks that have become a colophon for all of
China trace their origin to more than three hundred million years ago.
Water covered the area. The limestone peaks, called karst formations,
popped up as the crust of the earth moved. Time, wind, and water
sculpted the peaks. Trees and other foliage added the jade-green color.
Thousands of people over the centuries have molded the landscape
between and among the peaks into manicured plots that produce an
abundance of fruits and vegetables.

ALONG THE MAIN STREET of Guilin, a vendor sells remnants of animals for medicinal purposes.

A trip to Guilin is not only a sight-seeing excursion but a cultural one as well. A stroll through the dusty town, which, like most Chinese cities, is undergoing major reconstruction, affords the most interesting sights. Facial features as well as life-styles of different nationalities commingle. On the wide sidewalk along the main street, Zhongshan, are wire cages and plastic tubs containing a variety of creatures — turtles, snakes, pigeons, civets, and others we cannot identify. The animals are positioned on either side of restaurant doorways. They represent the restaurant's menu. Guaranteed fresh.

We were told about other exotic dishes in cages, including monkey, pangolins (resembling armadillos), and cats. Dogs are a delicacy. Such meals do not come cheaply. One menu listed turtle at 80 *yuan* ($21.62 U.S., excluding an automatic 10-percent service charge).

A few blocks away, a group of men were smoking and talking behind laundry hanging from clothes lines. In front of them was what turned out to be an exotic outdoor pharmacy. Displayed atop a blanket spread out on the ground were odd-shaped objects and small piles of powdery substances. These were remnants of animals. We could make out hooves of a deer, skulls, paws of a bear, claws, and pieces of bones. As I began snapping a photograph, one of the men, middle-aged, wearing a white T-shirt, with a cigarette in his right hand, ran over and shielded the objects from us. This was not a usual pharmacy, though the objects were for medicinal purposes. Government restrictions prohibit selling some of these items, and that was the reason for the objection to the camera.

Guilin is one of those towns that invites biking. Caves abound in the karst formations, and one of the most popular is the Ludi (or Reed Flute) Cave on the northwest outskirts of town. It is named for the reeds found at its entrance and which were once used to make flutes. The cave contains a vast grotto called the Crystal Palace that can accommodate one thousand people. In emergencies, area residents have used it as a refuge. Tour guides point out stalagmites and stalactites that resemble certain objects or about which legends have arisen. No matter how much I strained, my Western eyes could not pick out the "Castle and Dragon Crawling Around" or the "Mountain of Mushrooms and Hungry Tiger." Along the Li River, not far from downtown Guilin, is Elephant Hill. At the water's edge of Elephant Hill is a stone with a hole in it that extends out over the Li River and resembles, yes, an elephant's trunk. That I could see.

For all its unusual attractions, Guilin itself is not as scenic as its reputation maintains. Maybe because it stands in such marked contrast to the beauty of the surrounding peaks, Guilin seems drab. The atmosphere is distinctly tourist. The city's popularity has spawned illegal money changers and tour entrepreneurs, who swarm hotels and transportation centers.

Go to Guilin, we had been told, and you will be disappointed. Go farther, and you won't be. Raija and I took the advice. We decided to go to Yangshuo, a village along the Li River. The weather was rainy and cold, but in this area that is not something to complain about. The weather presents its own unique brush strokes, at once breathtaking and ever-changing.

The boat trip to Yangshuo takes about six hours and includes lunch. Guided tours take visitors to the wharf of Yangshuo, where they can shop for thirty minutes at a market and then parade into waiting buses for the bumpy, two-hour ride back to Guilin.

The boat trip itself is spectacular. Like a sparkling coil of jewelry, the river meanders among the karst formations. The graceful peaks

NEAR YANGSHUO, a farmer plows a
rice field with a water buffalo.

reach upward, while the clear waters turn them into rippling reflections. The challenge is to find the viewing angle that conjures up the
scenes suggested by the lilting names given to the peaks: Fighting-
Cocks Hills, Clean-Vase-Lying-in-the-River Hill, Yearning-for-Hus-
band Rock, Horses-Watching-on-Picture Hill, Celestial-Being-
Turned-Millstone, among others. The scenery truly is beautiful,
inspiring a poet, Han Yu (768–824), to write more than a thousand
years ago: "The river forms a green silk belt, the mountains are like
blue jade hairpins."

When you discover something like this, the urge is to cling to it as
long as possible. Raija and I decided to spend a couple nights in
Yangshuo. While the river trip offers rare beauty, the area in and
around Yangshuo is stunning, timeless, idyllic. The village is nestled
along the banks of the Li River among the limestone pinnacles, which
resemble what giant, scraggly dragon's teeth might look like. There is
a hotel as well as a few guest houses. Backpackers and others who
consider themselves travelers instead of tourists have carved out a
quiet, backwater haven.

Along village streets too narrow for cars, we found such restaurants as Tony's Place, Green Lotus Peak Wine House, Mother's Restaurant, Hilton Inn (the name is borrowed), and Napoleon Bar, which is described on the sign outside as "so lovely so charming that it will be remembered by all and written down in the phase of history with a glowing achievement in doing the business for the tourists."

On this day, in the gentle, warm rain, we made our way to the Yangshuo wharf and hired a boat to take us to Fuli, a tiny village east of Yangshuo. If the rain let up, we might be able to bike back. In a boat that could have accommodated several dozen people, we, with our bikes, were the only passengers. A family of three operated the plain, wooden boat. As we left Yangshuo behind, the scenery turned dreamlike. We were completely surrounded by peaks shrouded in misty veils. Tufts of clouds swirled around the tops of the peaks as though in fast forward, altering the images more quickly than the mind could register them. The sights permeated the senses just as the moisture penetrated the body.

Forty minutes later, we docked at Fuli. The relentless rain kept us in a sheltered pavilion, where we met others seeking a dry place. A man with two daughters joined us. So did a man with two roasted dogs, their bodies completely intact except for the legs broken off at the joints. He was carrying them on a shoulder pole, one dog at each end. Their bodies had been singed, and the white of the bared teeth, still clenched, stood out against the brown skin. The rain persisted. The bike ride back had to be abandoned. After an hour of people and dog watching, we grew weary and returned by boat to Yangshuo.

After drying off, we felt it was time to experience Yangshuo by night. If you like serenity, you'll love the nightlife. There is nothing going on. With one marvelous exception. For 3 *yuan* (81 cents U.S.), you can take in the cormorant show. It is worth the money.

At night we boarded a small tour boat and followed a fisherman on a long, slender bamboo boat with a basket aft and a light bulb fore to enable everyone, including presumably the long-necked and hook-billed birds, to see what was going on. The cormorants are fisher-birds. They each have a rope fastened at the neck. They swoop beneath the water, catch fish, and then are pulled in, their catch emptied into a basket. The rope around the neck prevents the cormorant from getting a meal. As our fisherman adroitly manipulated his four fisher-birds, and as the shadowy peaks glistened in the moonlit waters of the Li River, the rest of the world, for a short time at least, seemed far, far away.

We returned on a crowded bus to Guilin. It stopped frequently to pick up and discharge passengers. A man boarded with cackling chickens. An old woman climbed on carrying an armful of melons the size of cantaloupe. She sat near the back, placing her fruit on the floor. Before long the fruit was rolling back and forth the length of the bus. Passengers amused themselves by playing a gentle game of soccer with the melons. When the old woman's stop came, she walked along the aisle collecting her fruit from grinning passengers.

At one stop, an elderly man boarded. He groaned as he lifted a gunnysack up and into the bus. Suddenly a noise leaped from the sack. It was the yelp of a dog. Soon the bus was filled with the cries of the dog, but no one seemed to mind. And it did not bother us. It was a joy to be around a dog capable of yelping.

IV

四

22 CLASSROOM CHILL

Harold Hill, that smooth-talking, high-stepping city slicker out to make a fast buck from unsuspecting small-town folk, came to Beijing in the spring of 1987 as part of the first professional production of an American musical in China. American flags waved. River City's Mayor Shinn somberly intoned the Gettysburg Address.

In the Chinese rhetoric of the day, the event reeked of "bourgeois liberalism." And when flim-flamming Harold (played by Wang Xingna, an operatic tenor) bussed Marian the Librarian (played by ballet dancer Chen Ziaoqin), the stage of the Tianqiao Theater near the Temple of Heaven blushed with decadence.

How could this be taking place? Right here in Beijing City? American and Chinese flags whipping to and fro across the stage? Meredith Willson's popular musical, set in a small Iowa town in 1912, represented quintessential early-twentieth-century American bourgeois liberalism. The production, directed by Americans, translated into Chinese, and performed by Chinese, drew praise. Two writers for the *China Daily* (May 11, 1987) described the performance as "excellent, the singing almost perfect. And the acting and dancing, which were expected to be relatively weak because of the cast's lack of such training, didn't hamper them from turning the production into a success."

In China it is not easy to separate the real from the unreal. In this case it was plain. *The Music Man* was imaginary, a light-hearted fantasy transported briefly and whimsically from one culture to another. Though Raija and I enjoyed the production, events offstage throughout the country were occupying our attention. For while *The Music Man* — translated in Chinese as *The Musical Instrument Peddler* — was attracting large crowds, other developments, including those in my

161

classroom, were bumping head-on into another kind of Chinese reality.

This was the post-student-demonstrations period. Almost daily new regulations were announced. The State Education Commission said special attention should be given to "political, ideological and moral qualities" of candidates being considered for admission to the nation's universities and colleges. A Japanese journalist, Shuitsu Henmi, was charged with buying state secrets and ordered to leave the country—the third journalist in ten months to be expelled from China. University and college students received instructions on how to spend summers and holidays to help them stay in touch with "workers, farmers and reality." A newly formed State Media and Public Office announced new criteria that all publications had to meet, including having "a clear-cut purpose in conformity with the four cardinal principles and serving the building of a socialist society." Surveillance of foreigners increased, and most people—teachers and students, foreigners and Chinese alike—became more cautious about what they said and did.

The new reality also seeped into my classroom. Until now, the effects of the government's attacks on bourgeois liberalization had not affected my teaching. Students and I had discussed the situation at the start of the second semester and agreed to continue in the manner of the first semester. There was the one requirement of having authorities check student-written articles that might be sent abroad for possible publication, but I did not consider that a serious intrusion. I felt the procedure might even help students avoid future trouble in their young professional lives.

Perhaps it was inevitable that the restrictions would catch up with me, though I did not consciously push to test the outer limits of tolerance. That was not my role here. Triggering what turned out to become the incident was a mundane, even routine, request I made of students near the end of the first semester in January. I asked them to evaluate the course and offer suggestions for improvement. Several mentioned they would like to have journalists come to class and tell about their work. They meant Western journalists, because they had ample opportunity to meet with Chinese journalists.

So at the start of the second semester, I called Mark Hopkins of the Voice of America and Ed Gargan of the *New York Times*, the replacement for that paper's John Burns, who was expelled from China in 1986. Both agreed to come in April, Hopkins first.

My students were excited because, I discovered, Hopkins was a media celebrity in China. The students were among the millions who listen to the VOA, partly to improve their English, partly to find out what is going on. Hopkins also, as any VOA listener in Asia could attest, had covered the 1986–1987 Chinese student demonstrations in a typically aggressive American journalistic style. Government officials had not liked it. They not only criticized the VOA's coverage but also accused the U.S.-government-run station of encouraging student unrest through its coverage.

Aware of the possibly sensitive nature of the classroom visits, I sought and was given permission for the two journalists to talk to my class. I was told there would be no problem.

On the morning of Hopkins' scheduled appearance, the students' behavior seemed odd. Several came to class late. Tardiness for these students was unusual; absence, rare. As we began reviewing papers I had corrected, the students seemed diffident, disinterested. I said we had to get on with the business because Mark Hopkins would be here soon. They sat up in their chairs, several rubbing the sleep from their eyes as if they had suddenly been jolted awake.

"He's not coming," said Ding Liguo, the student from the city of Hangzhou, who was spokesperson for the class. He went on, "The visit has been canceled."

"Oh," I blurted. "I wasn't aware of that. Are you sure? No one told me."

I was stumbling for words, trying to sort out what was taking place. Indeed, no one had told me about any cancelation. Or, at least, not that I could remember. Communicating subtly or indirectly, I was aware, was standard Chinese practice. Maybe I had missed a signal somewhere.

I was shocked to learn that students had been told Hopkins's visit had been canceled. They even thought I had been instructed to cancel the visit. But through misunderstanding or miscommunication, I had not gotten the message. An institute official actually had telephoned me two days earlier. I thought it was to welcome me back from a lecture trip I had made to Shanghai. After hanging up the phone, I had mused to Raija, "I wonder what the purpose of that call was," and then had forgotten about it. Everyone, it seemed, knew the lecture was canceled with the exception of two people—Mark Hopkins and me.

As I tried to unravel the confusion, 9:30 a.m. was approaching. That was the time Hopkins—at least as far as I knew—was to enter the classroom. We were to meet his car at 9:15 at the entrance to the

People's Daily. I asked Ding Liguo to meet him and escort him to class. Ding Liguo still insisted Hopkins would not be there.

"You may be right," I said. "But just in case he does show up, someone should be there." Off he went with a classmate.

An institute official noticed the flurry of activity in the classroom and came in. He also told me Hopkins's visit had been canceled. Further, did not I remember our telephone conversation two days ago? Whoa. Apparently I had been told to cancel the visit. Obviously I had not. Clearly we had not communicated. I said that as far as I knew the visit had not been canceled and that Hopkins might walk into the classroom any minute. The official was flustered, and I prepared for the worst by asking, "If he shows up, should we shut the door? Should we politely tell him about the misunderstanding? Or should we let him go ahead?"

While we sifted through the options, anxiety mounted with each minute's tick toward 9:30. At this point, I almost hoped Hopkins would not show up. But he did. On cue. Just like a broadcast journalist. Now it was face-saving time. Since it would have been embarrassing to turn Hopkins away, he was permitted to talk to students. His remarks ranged from coverage of the student demonstrations to differing press philosophies, provoking one of the liveliest class discussions of the year.

In the United States, Hopkins is relatively unknown as a journalist. In China, as chief of the three-person Beijing Bureau of the VOA, he was on a par with Tom Brokaw and Dan Rather combined. Estimated listenership ratings gave him a small fraction of the potential audience, but that was enough to amount to 20.5 million listeners. Students treated him like a celebrity. Most Americans know little or nothing about the VOA because the station, under its charter, cannot broadcast in the United States. But for much of the rest of the world, including especially the Chinese, the VOA is a regular short-wave radio companion that helps them improve their English and often tells them things about the world and their own country they might not hear otherwise.

Hopkins told students that the Western media saw the 1986–1987 demonstrations as "a major political event." For a time, the VOA provided many Chinese with their only news of these events. The Chinese media did not begin reporting the story until December 20, after the Shanghai demonstrations had begun.

The VOA's coverage had its flaws—such as unverified estimates of crowd sizes and numbers of those arrested — but the station could not be faulted for lack of timeliness. While stories raged about the future of Hu Yaobang, who finally resigned as Communist party general secretary, the VOA was carrying cautious reports of the rumors. When the government news agency, Xinhua, finally broke the story at 7 p.m. January 16, Hopkins had a line open to Washington, D.C., from which all VOA programming originates. Five-and-a-half minutes after 7 p.m., the VOA was sending the story around the world. Later, China's Ministry of Foreign Affairs criticized the VOA for its "biased, inaccurate and distorted coverage" of the demonstrations.

Hopkins, at age fifty-five, short, stocky, and graying, was not only professional but professorial. He strolled about the classroom, answering questions candidly and with ease. Occasionally he punctuated his answers with the dark, horn-rimmed glasses he shifted from hand to hand. The students listened and asked questions in rapt attention. It was, said one student, "like finally meeting an old friend."

Hopkins said one reason Chinese listeners followed the VOA's coverage so closely was that the Chinese media were so slow in their own coverage. "The Chinese government's view at first was that if you don't pay attention, the student demonstrations will go away," he said. "Xinhua's coverage was too late with too little. The government never gained credibility with the students."

Some might regard Hopkins as a public relations voice for the U.S. government, but most listeners of the VOA would disagree. This is not to say the VOA, which has more than one hundred transmitters worldwide and a 1987 budget of more than $150 million, is an independent source of information.

"To a certain extent," Hopkins told the students, "all news organizations propagate a point of view. We're all in a sense propagandists. The Western approach is to find the flaws — that may be our bias." He admitted the VOA does not cover the flaws of the U.S. government the way the regular American press does.

Hopkins, born in Peoria, Illinois, is a seasoned journalist. He began his career on a weekly newspaper and then spent ten years with the *Milwaukee Journal.* He worked as a correspondent in the Soviet Union and wrote a well-received book about the Soviet press (*Mass Media in the Soviet Union,* published in 1970). He traveled extensively in the Soviet Union in the 1960s and has received peer recognition for his work, including a citation from the Overseas Press Club. After two years of studying Chinese, he went to China in July 1984.

"What's been the biggest problem during your three years in China?" a student asked.

"The difficulty of getting into the Chinese mind. Sometimes we [journalists] feel we can't completely understand the Chinese point of view." His response, I felt, was understated.

Afterward, students crowded around Hopkins to have pictures taken with him. They asked questions well into lunchtime, normally a closely protected time for the Chinese.

Hopkins's visit stimulated discussion for several class meetings. By no means did students accept or agree with everything he said. In particular, they questioned the Western concept of news and its emphasis on conflict. They also did not agree with his comment that journalists are not responsible for the outcomes or consequences of the news they report. These are issues that American journalism students and professors also debate.

After Hopkins left, I found a note on my desk. On Wednesday I was to see the institute director. There were to be no more such visits, I was told.

What about Ed Gargan, scheduled for next week?

"Postpone indefinitely."

By now I could translate "indefinitely" into Chinese usage. It meant "cancel."

The result of the entire incident, as probably any teacher already knows, was all too predictable: stagnation in the classroom. Neither students nor I could regain the enthusiasm for learning that we had had before.

How could this happen, especially with *The Music Man* a few miles away drawing rave reviews? As usual, I strained to understand. It had become clear that fallout from the student demonstrations of December and January was continuing and even intensifying. It was clear too, from a larger perspective, that the Chinese leadership was conducting several balancing acts simultaneously. One was maintenance of national stability while continuing the march of economic development. Another was keeping the door open to the West but being more selective about what was admitted. In addition, China was simply a land of contradictions. Political winds blow in several directions at once. People become wary. Being able to regulate uncertainty is its own method of control.

My classroom—involving, as it did, future journalists of the nation—may not have been typical of what was happening in China, but it was illustrative. It was not easy for me to explain to the students that no more Western journalists would be coming to class. Yet I suspected they understood better than I did.

One dejected and apologetic student reiterated the obvious: "China these days takes one step backward for every two forward."

Later, I learned that some students were worried about the story I had required them to do on Hopkins's classroom visit. It was intended merely as a reporting exercise and was to be an account of Hopkins's appearance. What would happen to their stories, they wondered.

Noting their concern and already pledged to do everything to avoid potential harm to their careers, I assured the students that only I would see the stories.

"Where are the stories?" a student asked. I was pleased at his journalistic skepticism.

"In my hotel room."

"Do you have an iron safe in your room?" shot back a student. Everyone laughed nervously at this.

"The papers are in a messy closet, and I'm not sure I can even find them anymore." I laughed nervously.

The chill pervading the country had invaded my classroom. Openness, trust, and intellectual exploration were giving way to suppression, suspicion, and caution. Perhaps the students would disagree. They were able to take events in stride. They had understanding where I had ignorance, and experience where I had none. They were also more accepting than I was. There was no other way for them to be.

23 HEROES

In January 1987, a twenty-six-year-old soldier who had lost his left leg fighting in China's nearly ten-year-old border war with Vietnam appeared in his wheelchair on a national television program celebrating the Chinese New Year. He sang a popular new song titled "Our Spirit is Dyed with Blood." His name was Xu Liang.

Xu Liang was to travel extensively in China speaking to young people. In the aftermath of student unrest, Xu Liang was to be a new hero for young people clamoring for more and quicker social change. For a short time, Xu Liang was to exemplify the values and dedication the government was trying to cultivate. He was, it seemed, one of the government's direct responses to the student unrest. Xu Liang was self-sacrificing, humble, articulate.

Asked about his television appearance, Xu Liang was quoted as saying, "When I received an invitation to sing on the New Year's program, I wrote back saying that if they wanted to promote me, I was not interested. I am just one of many soldiers from Lao Mountain (a battlefield on the Chinese-Vietnamese border). When I look at medals, I often feel guilty thinking of my comrades buried at the front. But if they want me to go and represent all soldiers with my singing, then I am more than willing. I would use all my heart to sing. I want to explore in the company of all young people: how can we develop and mature?"

Asked if he had joined the military to achieve fame quickly, he responded: "A woman university student asked me that recently. I said to her, in jest, 'Let's strike a deal here. I'll give you my medal of valour if you will cut off your left leg. Is that a fair swap? Do you want to take that shortcut?'"

Xu Liang was the latest in a line of government-inspired heroes designed to foster a nationalistic spirit in the citizenry. A forerunner was another highly publicized soldier, Lei Feng. Lei Feng died ingloriously in 1962 in an automobile accident, but he was revived as a model soldier—selfless, an example of "revolutionary heroism," a great proletarian hero. Here was an ordinary citizen in an ordinary job making an extraordinary contribution to his nation. Mao Zedong had issued the call: The whole nation should learn from Lei Feng. The slogan became "Learn from Comrade Lei Feng." Lei's beatification came about as a result of his unflagging loyalty to the nation's political system as expressed in a diary. A famous line from the diary says, "My only ambition is to be a rustless screw in the wheel of socialism."

These "model heroes" may seem strange to the Western mind. They have been chosen by authorities to serve as exemplars of sanctioned attitudes and behavior. It is a Chinese tradition to direct behavior by pointing to appropriate models, and China's leaders can make or break heroes overnight. In the West, heroes emerge not from governments but from mass media and private agents of promotion. Thus, according to polls in the United States, such people as Clint Eastwood, Michael Jackson, Mother Teresa, Jackie Kennedy, John Kennedy, Jonas Salk, Mickey Mantle, and others glide into and out of the heroic limelight.

Did my students regard military hero Xu Liang as their hero? I wondered about that. No one ever spoke of him. Nor, it occurred to me, had students mentioned individuals whom they held in particularly high regard. Who were the heroes of my students? Who reflected their values, their visions and hopes for the future? Who inspired them? Maybe the Cultural Revolution in its aftermath had denied them heroes.

A nation's heroes tell something about the values of the nation, and a person's heroes cannot help but tell something about the values of the person. As Jonathan Swift put it in "Cadenus and Vanessa" more than two hundred years ago, "Whoe'er excels in what we prize, Appears a Hero to our Eyes."

To me, many of my students themselves seemed like heroes. Despite the constraints under which they lived and the frequent experience of having high hopes dashed by bitter disappointment, they constantly amazed me by their resiliency and their devotion to China. They spoke ardently about wanting to improve the country. They wanted the chance to contribute their share to national development. Several had overcome great handicaps to get to this classroom. Some talked about overcoming the deadening effect of the Cultural Revolution or surmounting some family obstacle to teach themselves academic subjects and to learn English on their own. They called it "self-study," and it had made a difference in their lives.

Perhaps massive governmental campaigns are responsible for this spirit. But then it was obvious that such campaigns do not always have the desired effect. Some Chinese today scoff at the stories about Lei Feng. Some no doubt made fun of Xu Liang. The reason involves the changes that have been taking place in China. Propaganda does not find such easy prey as it did before the changes.

Nonetheless, there is a national, even patriotic, spirit evident in China. It struck me as a culturally embedded trait that simply came from being part of one of the world's oldest continuous civilizations. Regardless of its origin, the feeling was strong among my students and many other young people I met that citizens ought to persevere and sacrifice and strive toward national goals, which at this time centered on modernization and development of the nation.

"Who are your students' heroes?" I was asked by James O. Freedman, who came to Beijing in the spring as head of a University of Iowa delegation to promote faculty and student exchange programs. We were in a taxi traveling on the eastern section of Andingmen Avenue, a major thoroughfare in the north of Beijing near the Lama Temple.

"I'm not sure," I had to reply. "I suppose Deng Xiaoping. Maybe, for a few, Mao, though he's generally out of favor."

One day in class I brought up the subject of heroes. Students asked me if I had one, and I told them Albert Schweitzer. They had heard of the multitalented doctor, who was born in Alsace, then under German rule, and who had set up medical care facilities in French Equatorial Africa, now within the Republic of Gabon. Besides telling students about Schweitzer's accomplishments as an author, musician, and physician, I cited his humility. Once, riding a train in Europe, Schweitzer was asked why he was riding in third class. "Because there's no fourth class," was Schweitzer's response. The story amused the students. Maybe it was apocryphal. I do not know. But I like to think it was true even if it was not. I had never thought of a slogan like "Learn from Schweitzer." But maybe my own culture had imposed upon me my heroes. How could it be otherwise? In fact, what is "otherwise"?

The topic and the discussion about heroes suggested a writing assignment. I asked students to write brief essays on their heroes and give reasons for their selections. Not a scientific poll, to be sure. In fact, I had come across one such poll in China in which high school seniors were asked whom they admired most. The late Premier Zhou Enlai, who died in early 1976, was ranked ahead of Deng Xiaoping, who was their second choice, and British Prime Minister Margaret Thatcher, who came in third. All were rated far ahead of Mao Zedong.

I was in for a shock on this assignment. There was almost no agreement among the students. Only two came up with the same response — that they had no heroes. So much for the "mass line."

One student, in her early twenties, with a vivacious personality and infectious sense of humor, turned unusually serious in this assignment. She wrote that she remembered as a child being told stories of heroes. Sometimes she had wept when the hero died for others. This was the sort of hero she would like to be: "to die a glorious death for others' happiness." But then, two years ago, she recalled, a university student died while saving the life of a street cleaner. Was the student a hero? Some people said that if the college student were alive, he could contribute more to the country than would the street cleaner. So the person who sacrificed his life was not a hero. "I thought," continued the student in her essay, "my life is valuable; I should not sacrifice it at random. So I removed lots of heroes from my heart." Her conclusion was melancholy: "Maybe, some day later, I will find heroes again. But at present, I have no heroes."

Another student wrote that he had been searching "for some example for me to follow in my life but I failed." He wanted to become a pianist but could not afford a piano or a teacher. He thought about becoming a famous body builder but lacked the necessary training equipment and nutritious food. Finally, he asked, "Why not regard everybody around you as a hero? A combination of everybody's strong points would serve as the best example for me to follow."

Three students pointed to Chinese political leaders as their heroes:

—Deng Xiaoping: "A hero, it seems to me, should do something beneficial to people. Deng is one of this kind."
—Mao: "To Chinese, Mao is not a human being. He is the God of the nation. Without Mao, there would be no China." [This worship on the part of the student obviously was not shared by others. Mao's "hero" stock has gone down in China and continues to drop as events that took place during his leadership are re-evaluated.]

—Zhou Enlai: He was "considerate, resourceful and, most of all, in my opinion, kind to people—from the No. 1 leader in the country to the 'small potato.' A person like Mao also was great, but such a person needs a Zhou Enlai."

Most students found their heroes among friends and relatives. Two listed parents. Another wrote about one of his former roommates, a soldier who wept for his dead comrades when he was decorated for bravery. Another student wrote about a classmate—someone in our class, in fact—who had overcome personal hardship to be able to study journalism. Yet another mentioned a thirty-seven-year-old cousin who had made the pilgrimage on foot from Shanghai to Shaoshan (a village in Hunan Province where Mao was born and which during the height of the Cultural Revolution is said to have attracted three million pilgrims a year) and who had spent eleven years as a volunteer worker in Tibet. "I want to be as brave as her," wrote the male student.

Other heroes mentioned included a German language teacher at Ningxia University, who worked to "advance democracy and freedom in China"; a "go" (*weiqi*) chess player, who helped defeat top Japanese players; Meryl Streep, who is "the best actress in the world"; Carl Bernstein, who "braved many difficulties to unravel the Watergate scandal"; and a Chinese dancer, who, despite legs considered to be too short to excel at dancing, demonstrated that "determination and persistent pursuit can turn one's inferiority into superiority in life."

One student said her hero was the author Ba Jin (who turned eighty-five in 1989). The reason, she said, was that Ba Jin in his writing refused to blame others for the Cultural Revolution but freely confessed his own guilt. In a postscript to his five-volume collection of essays and articles, *Sundry Thoughts,* published from 1978 to 1986, Ba Jin wrote: "The 10-year calamity taught people to be silent, but the 10-year blood debts force the silent people to cry out. I have a bellyful of words and a bellyful of wrath, together with a bag of bones that have gone through the hell of the 'cultural revolution'." The student was old enough to remember the full impact of the Cultural Revolution on her life.

One student wrote that her hero was God. For it was God, she wrote, who symbolically helped people cope with disappointment and suffering.

Another student declined to name names but said that she admired "crusaders or social reformers . . . sons and daughters of the

Chinese people who fought for the liberation of their motherland during the dark days when China was under the exploitation, suppression or invasion of imperialist countries."

And, finally, one student wrote that during his twenty-eight years he had come to admire increasingly "those who are ordinary people but lead extraordinary lives."

We should probably not make too much of this hero business. To a large extent, the heroes of the students reflected the human range of hope and despair, of aspiration and disappointment. The lack of agreement may have signified personal uncertainty about the future, which is by no means a culturally unique phenomenon, or perhaps confusion about the next steps in the nation's modernization drive. But something else seemed evident: the people themselves — not governments or government officials — ultimately determine heroes.

24 CONFUCIUS'S
RELATIVES

Through the throngs of people, we shouldered our way through the gate and into the temple courtyards that kept leading through more gates and into more courtyards. Lining the pathway were tall pines, twisting cypresses, and stone tablets recording the history of the place. The temple complex, including its north-south axis, suggested on a smaller scale the architecture of the Forbidden City in Beijing.

Finally, just beyond the Gate of Great Achievements, was the place we were looking for. The sun's rays through the trees sprayed a dappled design on the two tiers of the reddish orange roof. A pavilion called Apricot Altar was the center of our attention. At this spot an apricot tree once stood. Confucius taught in the shade of that tree.

Legend also has it that a robust juniper tree nearby was planted by Confucius himself. Actually the tree is said to have been grown through regeneration of roots from the tree originally planted by Confucius. This distant and tenuous historical link does not diminish the significance of a visit to Qufu, hometown of the person who is probably China's most famous citizen.

All around this small country town of fifty thousand are ghostly reminders of one of history's most influential scholars. On these dusty streets in the Shandong Province of east central China, Confucius walked. Here he grew up, left, returned to teach, and died in poverty. He is buried on the outskirts of town. At the time of Confucius's death in 479 B.C., Socrates, the Greek philosopher, had not yet been born, and Sophocles, the Greek dramatist, was a teenager.

Now, two thousand years later, after being denounced in China's Cultural Revolution, Confucius and the "ism" that is his legacy are receiving renewed attention. Part of the rehabilitation comes from the prospects of luring tourists. Souvenir vendors around the Temple of Confucius hawk trinkets, T-shirts, and sunhats. But the renewed attention also derives from an attempt by authorities to recover certain elements in Confucian philosophy that, in a curious twist, might be useful in China's drive toward modernization.

As the nation develops its economy, partly through selective adoption of Western practices, the government has seen a need to develop an ethical or moral system — not as a religion but as part of an ideology — to regulate human relationships, including business. With awe and envy, the Chinese have watched neighboring Hong Kong, Singapore, and Seoul prosper. Maybe there is a kind of Confucian capitalism. At any rate, the Chinese are reexamining — critically — Confucianism for guidance.

Another indication of Confucius's current popularity is the number of persons who claim to be his descendants. One of every five Qufu residents — that's about ten thousand — claim to be related to Confucius. The number was substantially lower during the Cultural Revolution, when many "relatives" disavowed any ties for purposes of personal safety. It was during this period that the infamous Red Guards destroyed or defaced many Chinese temples, art relics, and monuments, all of which were considered tied to exploitation, capitalism, and feudalism. Qufu too felt the wrath of the Red Guards. It was predictable that Confucius, the first teacher in China to make a living from his teaching, would be vilified, for he epitomized not only old ways but also the intellectual community. In recent years, the government has poured money into restoration of the historic sites.

Raija and I visited Qufu with a group of foreign experts over the first weekend in May. It was not easy getting to Qufu. We took an overnight train from Beijing to Yanzhou and then a bus the remaining seven miles. The visit was part of a three-day outing that took us by bus north out of Qufu to Tai Shan, then to the city of Jinan and, finally, by overnight train back to Beijing.

Qufu teemed with Chinese people who had come to pay respects to the memory of the great philosopher. The throngs were there partly because this was May Day, China's third most important holiday behind Spring Festival (the Chinese Lunar New Year) and National Day on October 1.

Qufu's sole attraction is Confucius — that is, those sites associated with his life: the Mansions, or home; the temple complex; and the cemetery. The Mansions, a few minutes' walk from a new hotel, the Queli, is a labyrinth of pavilions, halls, and gardens. Here Confucius's descendants — the family name is Kong, a Latinization of Confucius — lived like emperors. Outside one of the kitchen buildings hangs a sign noting Confucian wisdom in food preparation: "The more careful choise of materials, the better, the finer the cutling and choping, the more desirable." Even philosophers need editors.

A short walk from the Mansions is the Hall of Great Achievements, or Dacheng Temple, the main structure in the complex. Outside, leaning against a wire mesh protecting exquisitely carved dragons coiled around stone columns, was an old couple. He, with a Mao cap and scraggly, white mustache and beard, and she, wooden cane in hand and black slippers on bound feet, were enthusiastically conversing with passers-by. Inside the temple is a newly restored statue of Confucius, an earlier rendition having been destroyed by the Red Guards.

A forty-minute walk north brought us to the Confucius Cemetery. It sits in the midst of the largest human-made forest in China and is among the finest preserved cemeteries in the country. Scattered through the forest of twenty thousand pines and cypresses are numerous temples and hundreds of grave markers and sculptures. Two gravestone tablets — one from the Song dynasty (960–1279) and another from the Qing dynasty (1644–1911) — stand in front of a grassy mound where Confucius is buried. It is a popular site for photos.

China's past always has a way of struggling with its present, and such was the case on this day. A few steps from Confucius's grave site, and attracting as much attention, was an old, white-bearded man in a white tunic, looking beatific and befriending tourists. He was eighty-one, and he claimed to be a relative of Confucius, seventy-three generations removed. This seems unlikely. The last known descendant of the seventy-seventh generation of the Kong family, Kong Decheng, fled to Taiwan in 1948. His departure is said to have ended a twenty-five-hundred-year chain of the family's residency in Qufu.

During his lifetime (551–479 B.C.), Confucius was not very influential. His ideas of government — based on a hierarchical system of respect — did not catch on. But the strength of his ideas was recognized and developed by his disciples, including Mencius (371–289 B.C.), who lived nearby in Zouxian and became the first great Confucian philosopher.

In recent years, China has established a Confucian Foundation, research center, and research association and has published books on

THE ENTRANCE to Dacheng Temple in Qufu.

Confucius. In addition, international meetings are being arranged to discuss Confucian philosophy. The first such meeting was held in the fall of 1987 and was attended by about 120 scholars from a dozen different countries. The cosponsors were China's Confucian Foundation and Singapore's Southeast Asia Philosophy Research Institute.

Concerning the meeting, Xin Guanjie, vice-president of the Confucian Foundation, was quoted in the *China Daily* as saying: "Chinese historians are beginning to actively study ancient philosophies again by trying to make objective, scientific and practical analyses of historical figures and ideologies."

The debate about Confucius centers on the classic collision of morality and politics. Some scholars at the seminar credited such Confucian virtues as hard work, frugality, emphasis on family, and self-discipline as keys to economic development in Singapore and elsewhere. Such qualities, they argued, could be beneficial to the mainland. Yet others, concerned with the tenets of Marxism, maintained that Confucianism is feudalistic and incompatible with socialism.

Considered a religion by some, Confucianism is more a philosophy or code for living, embodying attributes long associated with Chinese culture: respect, selflessness, obedience, and harmony. To Westerners, such virtues may seem desirable but old-fashioned, or at least idealistic.

Respect is the essence of Confucian thought, mutual respect in all relationships — between son and father, wife and husband, citizen and official. Together with values of obedience and selflessness, a harmonious society is to emerge. Over the centuries, Confucianism has left a deep imprint on Chinese culture. It has managed to change and adapt to circumstances.

During the Cultural Revolution, Confucianism was deemed misguided and feudalistic. Its belief that superior virtues of ancestors provided an example for later generations was seen as a threat to existing authority. A popular slogan at the time was "Down with Confucianism."

Today's China seems to be searching for a moral or ethical base

AN EIGHTY-ONE-YEAR-OLD MAN is a center of attraction at Confucius Cemetery.

swept away by the Red Guards. Corruption seems widespread among officials despite government efforts to control it. If there is a predominant philosophy concerning human relationships in China today, it is probably something called *guanxi*. The term defies exact English translation; it means "relationship" or "building good relations" or "social capital." In practice, it amounts to mutual back-scratching, yet it is more than that. *Guanxi* tends to de-emphasize genuine human relationships and to stress linkages motivated solely by self-centered interests. It often means the need to present a gift to someone, even a public official, to get something done that the recipients presumably have an obligation to do anyway.

The practice of *guanxi* to us seemed akin to *zouhoumen*, which means literally "taking the back door," or circumventing the bureaucracy in some way. Thus, an acquaintance saw me as a "back door" when he asked me to intervene in his son's behalf to obtain an American visa to study abroad. I was not successful, but, happily, the visa came anyway.

Many foreign friends in Beijing expressed dismay over their inability to cultivate personal relationships with Chinese people. Previous experiences conditioned them to see any friendly overtures as immediately suspect: Okay, what does he or she want this time? The experience of a year in China hardly afforded sufficient basis to draw valid conclusions. Nonetheless, in our associations with many Chinese, Raija and I felt that frequently we were being used for some specific, often unstated, purpose. Actually, this did not bother us. We felt that if we could help people in some way—say, by writing a letter of recommendation or by acquiring a certain book—fine. We would have done the same anywhere. Occasionally, a blatant gift, such as the cloisonné vase that we received on one occasion, came uncomfortably close to bribery. Visitors to China, rebuffed and frustrated at the ineffectiveness of normal channels, occasionally emulated local custom. Once, on a tight schedule, we had to arrange a round-trip from Beijing to Xian on specific days. A friend of a friend managed to cash in on her *guanxi* and acquired the tickets.

To be sure, *guanxi* has universal and cross-cultural application. The practice is bound to flourish when goods are scarce and opportunities are limited. But one does wonder whether societies, or at least the kind of societies many people want, can exist on this basis. Confucius would have said no. His version of the Golden Rule was: "Do not do unto others what you would not have others do unto you." If the measure of the strength of an idea is its persistence, then Confucianism deserves the closer look the Chinese are giving it today.

Near Qufu lies Tai Shan, which has its own Confucian connection. Tai Shan is the most revered of five sacred mountains in China. Nestled at the base of the mountain is the town of Tai'an, which is about seven thousand steps from the top of the mountain. On this weekend, the mountain path was crowded with Chinese people making the pilgrimage to offer special prayers in the temples at the summit of Tai Shan.

Legend has it that if you can walk to the top you will live to be one hundred years old. Raija and I began the trek, but rain, cold weather, and fatigue drove us back. Undeterred were a number of old women slowly wending their way upward on bound feet. Since we did not get to the pinnacle, we cannot question the conclusion of Confucius who, upon reaching the top of Tai Shan, is said to have looked out and proclaimed: "The world is small." We may not reach one hundred, but we can still agree with Confucius.

25 COWBOYS

Inner Mongolia in the north of China is Genghis Khan land. It is also "big-sky country." Under a limitless blue, the plains seem to extend forever. Cowboys gallop by, usually on horseback but occasionally on camels.

The Mongols—somehow Westerners want to say "hordes"—are characterized historically as ruthless barbarians who built an empire by fighting on horseback. It was Genghis Khan (1162–1227) who brought the Mongols together after two decades of warfare, and it was he who in 1211 led an invasion of China that after two years finally broke through China's Great Wall. By 1279, one of Genghis's grandsons, Kublai Khan, had taken over all of China—the first and only time China has been ruled in its entirety by foreigners.

But the Mongolian conquests were short-lived. By the end of the 1300s, the entire Mongol empire had disintegrated. Today there are two Mongolias—Inner Mongolia, China's northern buffer with the Soviet Union, and Outer Mongolia, a republic dominated until recently by the Soviet Union. Inner Mongolia is one of China's five autonomous regions, which include Ningxia in the center, Guangxi in the south, Xinjiang in the north, and Tibet in the southwest. Large numbers of China's more than fifty minority groups live in the autonomous regions. Policies affecting the autonomous regions presumably provide for limited political autonomy and encourage maintaining the indigenous culture. People we spoke to, however, were hard-pressed to explain the difference between the nation's provinces and autonomous regions.

In early summer, Raija and I, together with our daughter Christa, who by now had joined us, took a three-day weekend trip to Inner Mongolia. As with much of China, the region has tried to promote tourism but with little apparent success. The main reason is

182

that Inner Mongolia does not really seem to be the China that visitors are interested in. Inner Mongolia, with about twenty-five hundred miles of common border with the Soviet Union, is off China's main paths.

Our trip from Beijing was on a small, Russian-built aircraft operated by the CAAC, China's government airline. It took one and one-half hours to get to the capital city, Hohhot. We returned by overnight train. From the air we could glimpse sections of the Great Wall clinging like a serpent to the green hills below.

"Good fences make good neighbors," someone mused in reference to Robert Frost's poem "Mending Wall." That reminded me of an article I had just read. It was written by an English professor, Michael S. Helfand of the University of Pittsburgh. The article was one of a number of papers presented during the year at Shanghai International Studies University. I was helping edit the papers for a book that was published in China under the title *Perspectives in American Studies: A Reader by American Scholars in China.* Helfand, who was in his second year of teaching in China, had written about a study of the interpretations made by both Chinese and American students of works by two American authors, including Frost's "Mending Wall." Chinese students felt the poem reflected a sense of togetherness and working together because, after all, the neighbors had come together to mend the wall. American students, on the other hand, saw the wall as symbolizing separation, a way of maintaining privacy. Seldom does research produce such clear results. Helfand argued that the different interpretations from the two perspectives show how cultures — themselves a result of symbol making — also teach us how to interpret.

Now, looking down on this Great Wall snaking gracefully along the contours of the Mongolian countryside, I could not help but contemplate its changing meaning. The Great Wall was erected with a purpose in mind — to keep out enemies. But that purpose has faded away. Yet portions of the Great Wall remain, and in fact, extensive restoration of faltering portions is under way. Walls are great metaphors for many things, but basically walls are meant to confine or to repel. It is not always clear which meaning is intended.

Few walls impinge on the wide-open spaces of Inner Mongolia. Away from the crowded streets of urban areas, Inner Mongolia reminds us that China is the third largest country in the world after the Soviet Union and Canada. The land has the feel of Wyoming or West Texas or Montana. It is China's land of the vanishing cowboy, and the people's nomadic way of life is giving way grudgingly, yet quickly, to the development of industry and exploitation of rich natural resources.

Hohhot, the capital, is a city of about 1.2 million and is the main entry point to Inner Mongolia. In Mongolian, Hohhot means "green town." In this arid region, it could well mean oasis. The Mongolians proudly sing about being "people on horseback" and assert that "our home is on horseback." But their nomadic life-style of roaming vast grasslands and living in yurts — portable housing units — has changed drastically in recent years. Horses are surrendering to machines. Horse riders are becoming factory workers.

According to the news agency Xinhua, Inner Mongolia forty years ago could not produce even a nail. Today it is one of China's leading producers of rare minerals, electrolytic aluminum, iron and steel, coal, timber, woolen textiles, milk products, and beet sugar.

Throughout 1987, the Chinese press published numerous articles about Inner Mongolia. This was because the government wanted to stress the success of its policies during the observance of the fortieth anniversary of the establishment of Inner Mongolia as an autonomous region. The main celebration occurred during the annual August 1 carnival, called *Nadamu,* meaning a traditional festival. It is a kind of Cheyenne Frontier Days during which Mongolians display their riding, archery, and wrestling skills.

For visitors, lodging affords curious and frustrating possibilities. In Hohhot, we stayed at the two-year-old Inner Mongolia Hotel, promoted as the city's only first-class hotel. It is that in appearance only, epitomizing two of China's contemporary problems: poor plumbing and poor management.

Among the highlights of Hohhot were several temples, a mosque, and the Museum of Inner Mongolia, with its magnificent statue of a flying horse on top symbolizing a spirit of looking forward. Unfortunately, the museum was closed while we were there. The temples were in sad condition, though restoration was under way. We found the busy streets in the old part of town most interesting. For sale were the famous Mongolian hot pots, in which, like Swiss fondue, thin strips of meat and vegetables are boiled in a bubbling broth and then dipped into spicy sauces.

In one stall along the street, a young man, sweating in a sleeveless shirt, shoved a piece of metal held by tongs into the glowing coals of a forge. He was a blacksmith. The shop reminded me of my own father's shop in Colorado, where, as a boy, I felt awed by his ability

TOURIST YURTS on the grasslands of Inner Mongolia.

not only to make horseshoes at a forge but to attach them to the hooves of usually stubborn horses. Around the corner was a small shoe shop. Inside, a man was making small, black-cloth shoes, actually slippers, which were displayed near the entrance on top of a wooden bench. We entered the shop and even thought about buying a pair of the slippers that were still being manufactured for the old Chinese women with bound feet. The man did not like our coming into his store and motioned for us to leave. We did.

The next day we set out by bus for the real Mongolia, the grassland. Three sections are open to visitors. We visited Ulantuge (sometimes spelled Wulantuge), which is the nearest of the three to Hohhot, about fifty-five miles north over the Daqing Mountains.

Our lodging here was a yurt, four persons to one yurt. The facility is round, like a wigwam, and about twenty feet across with no middle supporting beam. In former times, animal hides were wrapped around the wooden frame. Now felt tied with rope is used. The entire unit could be put up and taken down in much less time than it would take to find new rangeland for sheep. Not much can malfunction in a yurt.

The yurt we stayed in was mounted on a concrete foundation, which today's sheepherders and cowboys on the plains might have a hard time duplicating. Alert to tourist possibilities, the Chinese have attached to the tourist yurts metal huts with Western-style toilets. But at the outset we were told these facilities did not work. Thus, no unfulfilled expectation. Communal facilities sufficed.

After settling into our accommodations, we struck out in a bus over a dusty, barely visible trail to see an *aobao,* a three-tiered, circular stack of stones rising out of nowhere (in Mongolian *aobao,* sometimes spelled *obo,* means "to pile up"). The neatly stacked stones can be seen from a great distance in this nearly treeless land, and they help travelers get their directions. The sites also are used for worship, such as praying for rain, which usually is in short supply.

The tour included a stop at the grasslands home of a Mongolian couple who operated an animal husbandry farm. They did not live in a yurt but in an adobe-style structure. He was fifty-three, she fifty-nine. We crowded into what was their main living room. Sitting on a shelf were two plastic souvenir cups with pictures of the Statue of Liberty. The couple served us bowls of cow's milk, cookies, and dried goat cheese. The husband, attired in a handsome Mongolian suit, and the wife, wearing a long gown, graciously showed us their home and posed for pictures outdoors. This was an organized tour, and we had the distinct feeling that these scenes had been enacted many times before.

The couple told us they had six children — five boys and one girl. China's one-child policy, which is designed to control population, does not apply to national minority groups. In fact, the number of Mongolians living in Inner Mongolia has been a subject of close study by the Chinese. Today, according to government figures, the number is the highest throughout the history of this ethnic group — 2.85 million. Under Genghis Khan, the number was just over a million. At the time of the founding of the Inner Mongolia Autonomous Region in 1947, the number was less than a million. The number of Mongolians actually represents about a tenth of the total number of people in Inner Mongolia, which has a population of slightly more than 20 million. Once we saw the Mongolian features of dark, ruddy complexions, we became aware that we had seen few Mongolians in Hohhot. Most were Han Chinese, as distinguished from Mongol, Manchu, or other non-Chinese ethnic groups.

The Chinese government is eager to point to the progress that minority groups have realized under Chinese leadership. Government reports note that Mongolians have benefited enormously since becoming part of China forty years ago. For example, one astounding statistic—the veracity of which I could not confirm—is that the average life expectancy for Mongolians has increased during the past four decades from 19.6 years to 69.3.

Around the Ulantuge Commune, there was not much going on. Grazing herds of sheep were enough to excite visitors. Occasionally a Mongolian cowboy galloped on horseback out of nowhere into the commune. A few Bactrian camels were brought out for tourists to ride, and an exhibition was held of Mongolian wrestling, in which combatants wear leather vests and try to pull one another to the ground. Meals featured huge chunks of mutton served with chopsticks and a sharp knife.

In the commune, a lonely lama, or monk, held vigil at the Puhui Lamasery. The lamasery—a monastery—was once very busy, he said, but now few people come. He eagerly showed us the temple and was sad to see us leave. Before 1947 Inner Mongolia had eight hundred lamaseries. The number has declined to forty.

As for Genghis Khan, some claim his remains are in a mausoleum about 180 miles southwest of Hohhot. We did not get there.

It is clear that, as happened in America's own West, rapid change is coming to Inner Mongolia. Because of the rich natural resources, authorities have embarked on a plan to double the combined value of the region's industrial and agricultural output by 1990. For the nation as a whole, this will be another step forward in its modernization drive. For the Mongolians as a people, it will be another step away from their cultural heritage.

T ibet is surreal. It evokes images of the past and visions of a future, but the present intervenes. It is a place where religion rules people's lives, where mountains devoid of vegetation dip into lush valleys below, and where at 12,083 feet above sea level and gasping for breath, you feel you are standing on top of the world.

The Potala Palace, its golden roofs etched against a deep blue sky, seems suspended in midair above the city of Lhasa. Pilgrims, dressed in layers of colorful, thick, yak-smelling clothing, devoutly prostrate their bodies at the Jokhang Temple. Others walk clockwise, always clockwise, around the temple, continually cupping their hands together and bowing. In Barkhor Square, young monks in robes and broad-brimmed hats sit cross-legged, chanting and burning incense. Nearby in the bustling market, sellers and buyers haggle over the prices of everything from false teeth to yak meat. The sights are vivid, unreal, and, yes, like Shangri-la. But the impressions on the mind are, at least in part, illusory. Tibet is a troubled land. The reasons are historical and intrude into the present.

For one thing, the Tibetans' spiritual leader, the fourteenth Dalai Lama, is in self-imposed exile in India. He fled Tibet in 1959 during a rebellion against China's central government. He refuses to return for fear of being turned into a Beijing-based bureaucrat.

A closer look around Lhasa reveals thousands of Han Chinese. Han Chinese have been pouring into Tibet for several years as part of the Chinese government's policy to assist and influence the Tibetans. When we visited in July 1987, before the riots that took place the following fall and that have occurred intermittently since then, the Chinese presence already included an estimated quarter of a million troops. Tibet itself, according to Chinese figures, has a population of

THE POTALA PALACE stands like a jewel among barren peaks in Lhasa, Tibet. It is one of the architectural marvels of the world. The palace, with hundreds of rooms and shrines, is the former winter home of the Dalai Lama.

1.9 million, of whom several hundred thousand are Han Chinese.

Poverty is another problem for the Tibetans, who occupy one of China's five autonomous regions. Tibet has thirty-two million acres of grazing land and only a million acres of arable land. Per capita income is 412 *yuan* ($110 U.S.) as compared with the national average of 1,005 *yuan* ($270 U.S.). In a way, this figure is not very meaningful because it is hard to frame a suitable concept of poverty in Tibet. The people seem to be very poor when it comes to modern conveniences, such as telephones and bathrooms. But when it comes to the nonmaterial, the spiritual, the Tibetan people are among the richest in the world. By such standards, it is the West that is impoverished.

The problems that have beset Tibet are not easily identified, let alone explained. Raija, Christa, and I had the rare opportunity to visit Tibet as independent travelers. Our week-long visit took place

THE JOKHANG TEMPLE is one of Tibet's holiest shrines.

IN BARKHOR SQUARE monks, oblivi-
ous to the activity around them, practice
mudra, symbolic hand gestures used in
worship.

between briefer stops by Jimmy Carter and the West German chancel-
lor, Helmut Kohl. For us the trip was a chance to encounter, even for
a brief time, a land that is a mystery for the outside world. Why is
there this strange fascination for Tibet?

Our Boeing 707 alighted gently on a runway along the Lhasa
River amid hundreds of soaring peaks laced with mounds of fine sand
and sparse foliage. The air was dry, the temperature dog-days hot,
and the city of Lhasa a bumpy one-and-a-half-hour bus ride away.
Access to Tibet is limited. No train tracks lead to Lhasa, Tibet's
capital city. Overland travel, especially from Nepal, is popular but can
be treacherous. We met an intrepid New Zealander who had started
by bus from Nepal, changed to a jeep, and was forced to trek by foot
after landslides washed away the road as well as his luggage. He could
have turned back, but the lure of Lhasa was too great. Now he carried
all of his remaining traveling possessions in a small plastic shopping
bag.

Lifting even light luggage in this altitude induces instant fatigue and shortness of breath. Nearly every visitor, regardless of age or physical condition, experiences some altitude sickness. Symptoms included headaches, vomiting, and high fever. The remedies are simple: drink plenty of liquids (nonalcoholic), try some aspirin, and, most especially, take it easy. If this does not work, a person is in trouble. We paced our acclimatization, suffered only shortness of breath, and were pedaling bikes after a few days.

If you require lodging with Western amenities, the place to stay in Lhasa is the Lhasa Hotel, a United States–Chinese joint venture offering comfortable economy rooms at 40 *yuan* ($10 U.S.) per person. It is not as close to downtown as the Yak Hotel, but its Western Restaurant offers the "biggest yak burgers" in town, and the Chinese menu lists such Tibetan dishes as Yak Eyes (15 *yuan* or $4 U.S.) and Yak Belly Marinated with Curry (12 *yuan* or $3.25 U.S.).

The most striking feature of this land is its people. Dark-skinned, they resemble American Indians. Invariably, men, women, and children offer warm smiles to Westerners but not to the Han Chinese. Walking toward the Lhasa River late one afternoon, we met two Tibetan women, perhaps eighteen to twenty years of age. With her right hand, one woman reached out and clasped Raija's left hand. Unable to exchange a word, they walked to the river, communicating the entire way by swinging their arms and punctuating the silence with intermittent bursts of laughter. The innocence of it all was sensuous. We had the same feelings the day before when we saw two adult monks at the Lhasa Hotel. They had just arrived from the countryside, and, as though having just been blessed with sight and touch, they were closely examining a revolving glass door. The wonder of it all! I was sorry I could not remember the last time I was amazed at a revolving glass door.

Tibet traces its recorded history to the seventh century. China's claims go back to the thirteenth century, when both countries were incorporated into the Mongol empire. It was in 1950, a year after Mao Zedong had established the People's Republic of China, that China reannexed Tibet. Although some Chinese troops moved into Tibet in 1950, the Tibetans were permitted to maintain their social, political, and religious structures. But in 1959, an anti-Chinese rebellion broke out, resulting in great loss of life and the destruction of many temples and monasteries. The Dalai Lama fled to India. An estimated eighty thousand other Tibetans went to India and Nepal.

THE DESTRUCTION of religious statues in Norbulingka is a grim reminder of the Cultural Revolution.

Needless to say, the Tibetans are receptive neither to the authority of China nor to the presence of the Han Chinese. One day we were walking in the Norbulingka, formerly the Dalai Lama's summer residence, which is about two miles west of the Potala Palace. It was a depressing excursion. As we finished looking around the now-vacant summer home and began walking out, a guide called us over to a storage building about the size of a two-car garage. He pulled back a canvas curtain. Inside were piles and piles of the debris left from smashed and broken Buddha statues. We walked to the nearby small zoo. It was filthy, and the animals were thin and scrawny. Not far from the zoo we saw two young Tibetans, a man and a woman, working outdoors in the searing sun, cleaning and polishing small Buddha statues. The statues were lined up as if in a parade on wooden beams. The man knew some English.

After we had chatted awhile, I asked bluntly, "Do you like China?"

Unhesitatingly, he said, "No." Quickly and nervously, he looked around.

Evidence of the physical destruction of temples and monasteries during the Cultural Revolution was everywhere. Once Tibet had more than six thousand monasteries, and only a handful survive. As many as a million Tibetans also may have died during this period.

We did not have an opportunity to talk with many Tibetans, though they are usually eager to try their limited English, mostly limited to "hell-owe" and "how much." If they take a liking to you, they curl the tongue upward and stick it out at you. Many ask for photographs of the Dalai Lama by giving the thumbs-up sign. The pictorial treasure elicits profuse gratitude, sometimes accompanied by tears.

Women wear several layers of clothing that include colorfully striped aprons. They like silver jewelry with turquoise and orange coral. Men don heavy coats. Except for a few who have discovered "tennies," they wear multicolored felt boots. The women's black hair is braided or bunned. The hair customarily has 108 braids, the same number as the number of holy books in the Tibetan Buddhist canon. Standing out among the Tibetans are tall, husky men wearing high boots, a swirl of red yarn draped around their long black hair, and sheathed knives at their waists. They are *khampas,* famed as warriors.

Wherever we went in and around this city of 175,000, the Tibetans stood in contrast to the many Han Chinese and the many green-uniformed soldiers of China's PLA (People's Liberation Army). The

soldiers were at the main Tibetan congregating place, Barkhor
Market, which teems with people from throughout the region. Tibetans come here, some leading their sheep and donkeys, to worship at
the golden-roofed Jokhang Temple, one of Tibet's holiest shrines. The
market is a kaleidoscopic assemblage of humanity bordering on bedlam. Smoke from religious fires suffuses the area, and cripples and
beggars abound, their existence seemingly dependent on the generos-
ity of passers-by more fortunate than they.

Two monasteries—Drepung and Sera—lie three or four miles
outside town. En route to both sites, we noticed heavily camouflaged
military vehicles. And at both sites, we saw toppled buildings and
smashed statuary, sad reminders of the destruction that still scars this
land and its people.

Near the Sera Monastery, Tibetan "sky burials" take place. Because of the stone-hard land and the limited fertile soil, Tibetans have
adopted as one way of disposing of their dead the dissection of the
human body and the feeding of the entire remains to vultures. This
takes place during a solemn ceremony high in the mountains. A few
years ago visitors were permitted to observe the ritual. No longer. The
documentary film *Tibet* vividly depicts how a body is blessed,
wrapped in a cloth in a sitting position, and taken to a mountain site,
where it is cut into pieces and offered as food to birds of prey. The
bones, including the skull, are crushed and mixed with a kind a
ground barley called *tsampa,* and this too is consumed by the vultures.

In one room at the Sera Monastery, we came across two youngsters printing *sutras,* sacred Buddhist texts. The text was carved in
relief on a wood block placed on the floor between the two boys. One
youngster was in charge of the actual printing. He applied ink to the
block. The other placed parchment on the woodcut, and the first used
a rolling-pin-like device (called a brayer by printers) to make the
impression. The same steps were repeated to print on the reverse side.
Mastering this skill is important for novitiates.

The interiors of the monasteries and the temples reek with the
smell of yak butter. It is a rancid smell that seeps into clothing. In the
temples constant parades of monks carry yak butter and oil in metal
containers and spoon it into brass bowls with a wick floating in the
center. Ever-dependent on the faithful monks, the flickering candles
not only light the way but suggest the evanescent nature of life itself.

Because of the unique land and life-style of the Tibetans, China
since 1980 has encouraged tourism in the region. More than thirty

thousand visitors came in 1986, one third of them from the United States. Tourists bring not only fascination for a strange land but also foreign currency. As a result of the disturbances in the past several years, tourism has been curtailed.

The Chinese government has spent millions of *yuan* in restoration. According to official figures, from 1952 to 1986 the central government gave nearly 10 billion *yuan* ($2.7 billion U.S.) to help Tibet develop socially and economically. Projects have included educational and medical facilities as well as reconstruction. That investment, together with other governmental policies promoting the region, probably explains the ire of the Chinese when on June 18, 1987, the U.S. House of Representatives approved an amendment critical of China's treatment of Tibet. The amendment accused China of imposing rule over Tibet through military force since 1949 and of killing more than one million people in Tibet because of "political instability, imprisonment and widescale famine."

Stung by these charges, as well as by another amendment accusing the Chinese government of violating the human rights of its citizens, China reacted sharply. In Washington, D.C., and Beijing, Chinese officials denied the charges, pointing to progress that had been made and suggesting in typically polite and indirect fashion that the United States stay out of China's business.

Former U.S. president Jimmy Carter even got involved. A little more than a week after the U.S. House of Representatives approved the amendment, Carter and his wife Rosalynn visited Lhasa as guests of the Chinese government. They spent two days there. The front-page headline in the June 29, 1987, edition of the *China Daily* reflected the story's tone and the government's wish: "Carter sees the truth about Tibet."

Two days later, after a meeting with Chinese leader Deng Xiaoping, Carter called a news conference in Beijing and diplomatically (which means carefully) said remarks attributed to him were accurate in the context of comparing present conditions with those of the Cultural Revolution. But he added, "There is a long way to go before the freedom of the pre–Cultural Revolution stage is restored."

During the turbulent decade from 1966 to 1976, religion was outlawed but since has been restored. Prayer flags with sutras printed on them appear all over, suspended from buildings, strung on ropes, or attached to sticks. Prayer wheels likewise are everywhere. People carry small prayer wheels—metal cylinders with wooden handles, resembling baby rattles—and twirl them as they walk. At temples and monasteries, prayer wheels are cylinders three or four feet in height and are spun by pilgrims and monks walking past. Inside the prayer wheels are printed sutras. The prayer-wheel spinning symbolizes a recitation of the contents.

Another facet of the Tibet military story involves India. Since 1914 China and India have argued over possession of a sparsely populated land area between Tibet and northwest India called Arunachal Pradesh. Heavy troop buildups on both sides—three hundred thousand soldiers in all, according to some estimates—have produced tensions.

Perhaps because of the military activity, but probably also because of the rugged terrain, transportation into and out of Lhasa was irregular when we were there. Flights between Lhasa and Chengdu, the only point for Chinese air entry, were canceled for two days. Our suspicion, heightened by tight airport security, was that Chinese troops and equipment were using the airport. Since the fall of 1987, several clashes between Tibetan monks and Chinese police have resulted in as many as several hundred deaths. Since the first outbreak, travel into and out of Lhasa has been restricted.

Resolution of the Tibetan issue poses a dilemma for the Chinese government. To spur development and, as the Chinese say, to rid Tibet of feudalism would drastically alter and even wipe out a distinctive culture and life-style. Not to help the region develop and improve the lives of the Tibetans would slow the nation's modernization drive and represent abdication of national responsibility. This may be China's most serious contemporary problem: how to make one nation out of more than a billion people, who in their composition include more than fifty different minority nationalities.

The Chinese news media pay a lot of attention to Tibet, which also figured in the nation's anti–"bourgeois liberalization" campaign in February 1987. A prominent intellectual, Liu Xinwu, was dismissed from his post as editor of China's foremost literary journal, *People's Literature,* for publishing a two-part novel that "vilified the culture and customs of the Tibetans." Titled *Show the Coating of Your Tongue, or Nothingness,* the story was written by author Ma Jian and appeared in the first two 1987 issues of the publication. The novel dealt with incest and sexual abuse among Tibetans. People, including some we knew in Beijing, snapped up the issues, which became popular bootleg items.

Publication of the novel initially was denounced as a product of bourgeois liberalization. A few days later, Tang Dechang, a member of the Chinese Writers' Association, said that although the novel's publication was an inevitable result of the ideological trend toward bourgeois liberalization, "we do not mean that Liu Xinwu himself or the novella deliberately advocated bourgeois liberalization." The news agency Xinhua quoted Tang as saying that while publication of a poor literary work that hurt the feelings of a minority people was a mistake, it should not be treated the same as the case of noted investigative journalist Liu Binyan, one of three intellectuals accused of advocating bourgeois liberalization and expelled from the Communist party. The leading newspaper for intellectuals, the *Guangming Daily,* suggested that the anti–bourgeois liberalization campaign may have been carried too far. It commented that some "leading comrades" had become caught up in the anti–bourgeois liberalization struggle to the point that they linked it to such unrelated fields as population control, attempts to reforest the countryside, and people's showing up late for work.

Long after we had left, our fascination turned to admiration and sympathy for Tibet and its people. The land is harsh. Adversity seems to be a permanent part of the fragile culture. Somehow the Tibetans help to bring about a balance to a world that too often seems out of balance. It is a land of innocence, of harmony with nature, of respect for all living beings. It is a land of the material rendered ethereal.

27 WRITING
ON THE WALL

ummertime in Beijing. Nature's rays turned up the heat. Along the bike paths, ice cream vendors offered welcome relief. Our year-long visit was winding down, and in a few weeks we would be departing China. But there was still one place I had not visited in Beijing—Democracy Wall. I was not even sure exactly where it was, though as it turned out we had unknowingly biked and walked past the place often. I thought maybe the wall, or at least the idea of the wall, would yield some special meaning to me as I tried to assess the year of teaching journalism in a society vastly different from my own.

For a brief time during the winter of 1978 and spring of 1979, Democracy Wall had served as a dramatic symbol of free expression in China. More than three decades earlier, Chairman Mao himself had articulated a powerful slogan: "Let a hundred flowers blossom and a hundred schools of thought contend." Mao's campaign in the 1950s was an attempt to encourage diversity of thought by inviting criticism of the Communist party and the government. After a few months, criticism had become so harsh that the campaign was halted and the government punished those who, it alleged, had gone too far. Other "hundred flowers" campaigns had sprung up later, but each time such gusts of free expression had been short-lived.

The 1978–1979 free-expression campaign was noteworthy for its vigor and resulted in the establishment of Democracy Wall. The wall was a place where posters with all kinds of messages could be displayed, a place where leaflets could be distributed, a seedbed for "a hundred flowers." The liberalization campaign ended abruptly in December 1979, when the City of Beijing closed Democracy Wall be-

DEMOCRACY WALL, once at the center of China's "hundred flowers" movement, is now an exhibit area.

cause, it was said, a few people were abusing the privilege of using the wall. Outspoken critics were arrested and imprisoned. Today, a decade after the Democracy Wall movement, some of its leaders are still in prison. Among them is Wei Jingsheng, one of the most prominent and vociferous critics, who coined the phrase "the fifth modernization — democracy."

Because of its symbolic nature, I wanted to make a pilgrimage to the site of Democracy Wall, just as everyone who visits Beijing must make a trip outside the city to the Great Wall. I telephoned a friend at Radio Beijing, a reporter. He agreed to take me to the place. We met on our bikes in front of Radio Beijing. It took us only a few minutes to get to the south entrance of the large shopping street called Xidan. We parked our bikes and walked past the entrance to the street. The brick wall is just east of this south entrance and runs parallel to the main thoroughfare that bisects downtown Beijing. The wall is located behind a busy bus stop. It extends about one hundred yards and has an overhang protecting viewers from inclement weather.

Parades of youngsters guided by watchful grandparents were strolling past the glass-covered display cases, peering at a children's exhibit on science and technology. Science and technology had taken over Democracy Wall. A symbol of free expression had been converted to a symbol of scientific achievement. I could not help but wonder about the relationship between free expression and scientific achievement: how far or how long can the one proceed without the other?

As I gazed into the display cases, shielding my eyes to reduce the glare from the bright sun, I suddenly saw, as in a series of flashbacks, the year pass before me. In my mind's eye, this place mirrored my year of teaching and observing journalism. I had come to China with the intention of making some small contribution toward development of the nation's human resources. In turn, China had received me graciously.

My thoughts returned to December and Shanghai and a dank classroom on the campus of Fudan University. I was listening to a group of students in an international journalism class talk about ideas they were proposing for reporting assignments. They were graduate students, and their assignment was to generate stories that dealt with social issues and offered possibilities for investigative journalism.

One student was working on the problem of child-bride marriages in Fujian Province. The custom involved parents marrying off their children at an early age with the youngsters having no voice in the arrangements. The student did not know much about the practice but thought it was detrimental to society as well as to the individuals involved and wanted to expose the practice. Another student wanted to investigate prostitution in Shanghai. Everyone knew it existed. The problem with doing this story was how to carry out the research.

The effect of China's one-child policy on the personality and character of children was another student's topic. Since the policy went into effect in the late 1970s, the challenge has been how to deal with youngsters who have become objects of extraordinary attention from parents and grandparents. The "spoiled brats," as we call them, have become "little emperors" and "empresses," as the Chinese call them. Other topics dealt with the possible social violence being spawned by the popularity of martial arts, lessons that still can be learned from the experience of the Cultural Revolution, promiscuity on campuses, the increasing number of divorces, and the problem of university students trying to make money in the changing labor market and still being able to contribute to society.

I was feeling right at home. Students in journalism classes in the United States also deal with social problems, many of them similar to the topics these students were pursuing.

The class then discussed an article that had appeared recently in the *China Daily* about a growing problem in China — smoking. The cigarette manufacturing industry is immense in China. So is the market. Increasingly, smoking is being regarded as a serious social problem, notwithstanding Deng Xiaoping and his ever-present cigarette.

"Whose self-interest is at stake in the tobacco industry?" asked the instructor, Lu Ming, a bright and energetic young man who had studied at the East-West Center in Honolulu. "What are the economic benefits to society? What are the social costs?" He was pointing out some of the complex issues in a serious social problem. Such issues had to be dealt with in a comprehensive, interpretative report.

Again, the discussion could have taken place in any number of classrooms in the United States. The fact that the topics were being discussed in China by future journalists seemed particularly remarkable to me. Was it a period again of a "hundred flowers"? The answer would come within two weeks, when thousands of students massed on the streets of Shanghai clamoring for more freedom and more democracy. The aftermath of the student protests in Shanghai and elsewhere in China yielded the opposite results. Just as previous campaigns had been thwarted by authorities with counter campaigns opposing liberalization, this brief flurry of free expression would also be nipped.

As journalism students the world over discover, a nation's journalism is like other institutions in the society. It is bound by the culture and by political and economic constraints. My Chinese journalism students admired the American press system because journalism is independent of the government. In this way, they saw at least the possibility that journalists could monitor government activities and officials. But the students were critical of the American press too. They felt that economics limited freedom of expression, that the primary freedom was for making money, and that freedom of expression was secondary. In China, the tradition has been that the government and the Communist party control the press as well as expression generally.

As in so many spheres of life in contemporary China, change is creeping into journalism. A "hundred flowers" debate of sorts is taking place. It is linked to economic and, in part, to political changes.

IN DOWNTOWN BEIJING, young people examine periodicals being sold at an outdoor stand.

Among journalists, there is often confusion about what can and cannot be done. For the unwary practitioner, it can be a minefield. For the politically astute, it can be a stepping stone to a career.

In the debate, two general schools of thought have emerged (though the discussion has been muted since the June 1989 crackdown). One advocates major press reforms, declaring that the basic system and role of the press should be altered. A few of those pressing for such reform argue that at least a segment of the press ought not to be controlled by the government. The second approach calls for more modest changes, such as modernizing newswriting techniques and production methods.

My students and colleagues sensed that change in the role of the Chinese press was in the air. They were eager to get their hands on books dealing with press laws. China has been working to develop new press legislation. Both the nature of those laws and a possible redefinition of the role of the mass media have been part of a spirited debate for several years. Students also wanted books about public relations, advertising, business, and economic affairs reporting. Economic reforms were opening up and even requiring new areas of journalistic expertise.

Any change, of course, will have to be predicated on Marxism and Leninism. This means upholding the Chinese Communist party's four cardinal principles: Socialism, Marx-Lenin-Mao Zedong thought, leadership of the party, and dictatorship of the proletariat. The principles, to be sure, can be interpreted in a variety of ways, and therein lies the rationale for justifying change. Any change also must take into account the press's role in serving the nation's current modernization program in agriculture, industry, science and technology, and national defense.

The journalistic mission in China became vividly clear one day near the end of my teaching stint in Beijing. Entering the classroom, I noticed these words on the blackboard: "In politics great store will be set by disseminating the four cardinal principles." The words "great," "store," and "by" had been underlined. Was the message meant for me? Or for the students? Or was it merely left over from the previous afternoon's class? I never found out the answers to these questions.

Chinese students often asked me why the American press emphasizes negative or bad news. In dwelling on sex and crime and politics—"Irangate" was capturing headlines at the time—doesn't the press lower the morality of your society? Part of the problem, I explained, was confusion over cause and effect. The press, while contributing greatly to the shaping of social reality, is generally not responsible for bringing about the events that are covered. "Bad" news, I told them, does not disappear if it is not reported. In fact, a situation that provoked socially undesirable results could worsen if it did not receive attention from journalists. Curiously, as a result of my discussions with students, I became more critical of the American press system—its penchant for profits, its parochialism, and its obsession with events rather than processes—and at the same time more appreciative of what the American system offered, namely, another perspective on society and at least the possibility of diversity of information.

In China, Hu Yaobang, removed as party general secretary following the 1986–1987 student demonstrations, had presented a journalistic formula for coverage of good/bad news. Socially good news should get 80 percent of the attention; bad news, 20 percent. In the United States, the figures are probably reversed.

A perhaps trivial yet illustrative example of the difference between Chinese and Western journalism was provided in the fall of 1986, when Queen Elizabeth, accompanied by the Duke of Edinburgh, paid an official visit to Beijing and then toured the terra-cotta warrior museum in Xian. The *South China Morning Post* (October 17, 1986) had a seven-column headline datelined "Xian" across the top of page 1: "'But Beijing was ghastly,' says the Duke." The story quoted the Duke in a conversation with a group of British students studying Chinese in Xian. According to the story, he said if the students stayed away from Britain any longer, they would "go back with slitty eyes." The story acknowledged that the royal comments may have been made lightheartedly.

The Chinese press did not carry a word about the Duke's tactless, if not tacky, remarks. The reason, according to a Chinese teaching colleague who had studied in the United States, was that "we can't be sure the quotes are correct." And, she added, it would not serve to elevate the level of discussion.

Journalists in the West, of course, are always making similar judgments. What should be covered? What should be included? What should be left out? The really hard question becomes *why.* Why cover this? Why not cover that? The basis for such judgments are social, political, and economic, and these factors vary from one press system to another.

But as the Chinese have discovered, "bad" news does not disappear if it is ignored by the media. An example was the story of the student demonstrations. For several weeks, reports of these events came only from external media, including the VOA, the BBC, the Hong Kong newspapers distributed in China, and a few other publications such as *Time, Newsweek,* the Asian edition of the *Wall Street Journal,* and the *International Herald Tribune,* all of which usually were available in hotels and shops catering to foreign tourists. Weeks after the student demonstrations began, Chinese journalists finally were permitted to cover the story. The stories emphasized that most students were not demonstrating and that only a few troublemakers were responsible.

Although my main purpose in the classroom was to teach Western journalistic techniques and practices, occasionally and inevitably we wandered over into theory and philosophy. One class assignment involved viewing a movie on videotape and then writing an opinion piece about it. The movie was a dramatization of Norwegian playwright Henrik Ibsen's *An Enemy of the People* (1882). The story portrays the ethical dilemma of a physician and a journalist in informing the citizens of a health resort community about a deadly contaminant in the town's natural baths. The baths represent the economic life of the community. The physician, Dr. Stockmann, feels morally obligated to inform the citizenry about the health hazards of the baths, and in the process he opposes the community's established power structure, represented by the town's mayor and the newspaper publisher. There is another twist to the plot: the mayor and the physician are brothers.

Now the key question emerges: Should the public, that is, prospective patrons of the baths, be informed about this potential hazard? What about the town's economy? Is it absolutely certain that the baths represent a health threat? As with all Ibsen's plays, the questions carry a social universality and timelessness. In the play, Dr. Stockmann sacrifices everything, including career and reputation, for his convictions. The power structure prevails. The idealistic physician and his loyal family must face the town alone.

One student saw in the story a medical metaphor for journalism: "Mass media today should serve as a social 'microscope,' through which more people are able to see 'bacteria.'" Another wrote boldly: "We have had lots of 'Dr. Stockmanns' in China, and we need more." Then he added cautiously, "But we must remember there are many 'mayors' too."

Only one student did not see Dr. Stockmann as a hero. To this student, one of the older members of the class, the physician had lost credibility. People like Dr. Stockmann and his family members should not become social outcasts, she wrote, for then "they can't influence others any longer. . . . Their truth is useless." Recalling the Cultural Revolution, the student thoughtfully continued, "To force many other people to accept an idea, even if a truth, is always associated with revolution, sometimes even violent revolution. The result of a revolution is usually the rule of a tyrant, who often holds truth to win masses at the beginning and then abandons it. China's Cultural Revolution is an example. The 'absolute truth' later became 'absurdity.'"

In the spring, when blossoms were returning to Beijing, the effects of the clampdown on journalism after the student demonstrations were still being felt in my classroom. One student wanted to do a story about why the American television series "Little House on the Prairie" was so popular among the Chinese. The basic idea was fine, she was told by editors, but she should deal with a Chinese-produced program. Another student wrote a story in which "bourgeois liberalization" was mentioned. Editors deleted this reference. Of course, by then it was well known that Liu Binyan, the nation's premier investigative journalist, had been ousted from the Communist party and fired from his position with the *People's Daily,* the official organ of the Communist party.

Now, as midsummer heat radiated from the wall, the student demonstrations of December and January seemed lost to history. Men wearing tank tops and short-sleeve shirts walked slowly past the science and technology exhibits. One young man was shirtless. Grandmothers dutifully steered their young charges into the scant shade offered by a few trees. I strained to absorb the peaceful scene. If the sun is shining, as it was on this day, and if the youngsters stay for a while in one place, which they did, and if the glass windows are clean enough to yield reflections, as these were, then you can see eager, expectant young faces looking out at you from Democracy Wall.

After eleven months in China, our odyssey was near an end. The worst part was leaving the students. Nearly a year had passed since they had begun their graduate studies. I had been their professor, charged with introducing them to the fundamentals of journalistic news reporting and writing. In China a special bond develops between teacher and student. One student put it this way: "It's lucky for a young person to find a good spouse; it's luckier for a student to have a good teacher."

To these students, I had become *their* professor. In turn, they had become *my* students. At a farewell party, the students thanked me for teaching them. I thanked them for teaching me. The class presented me with a tapestry depicting the Great Wall. While changes swirl throughout China, the Great Wall stands firm and now epitomizes for me a special bonding with these students.

On an early Wednesday morning, a minibus arrived at the Friendship Hotel to take us to the Beijing Railway Station. Raija, Christa, and I had decided that we would leave China by train. Traveling north and then west would take us through Outer Mongolia, across Siberia, to Moscow, and eventually to Raija's home in Finland—Kurikka, a town about two hundred miles north of Helsinki. Our visit to China would culminate in a trip around the world.

The minibus was about twenty minutes late. The train was to depart at 7:40 a.m. We were nervous, though it seemed strange to be worrying about a few minutes when before long we would have the luxury of squandering minutes, even hours, since the train ride from Beijing to Moscow with no overnight stops takes six days.

Beijing's main railway station is a turbulent sea of humanity with the recurring movement of waves washing people in and out. Seeing

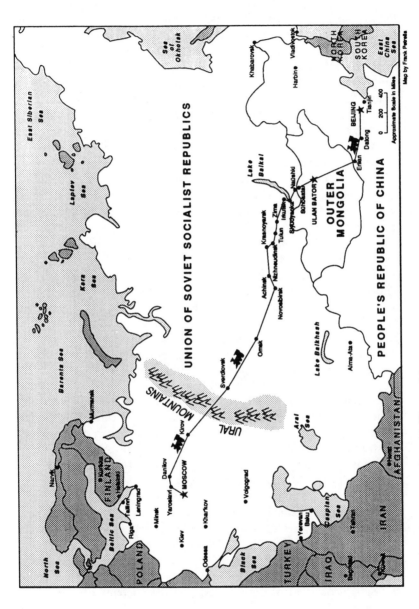

THE TRAIN ROUTE from Beijing to Moscow

us off were two members of the Institute of Journalism, a staff member of the foreign experts office of Xinhua, a friend from Radio Beijing, and one of my students, Zhang Xiaoquan, who once had brought us dumplings from the famous Goubuli restaurant in her hometown of Tianjin. Made of pork, spices, and gravy, the dumplings are tasty despite the name of the restaurant, which translates "dogs won't touch them." A colleague assured me the name simply meant that the restaurant was so highly regarded that it could get away with a name like that. We snapped the obligatory photographs, using as a backdrop the handsome green cars of the Chinese train that was to be our home across the grasslands of Mongolia, the expanse of Siberia, and the grandeur of the Ural Mountains.

We said our sad good-byes and thank-yous, and as we settled into the compartment with berths 29, 30, and 31 of car No. 4, the Trans-Mongolian International Express departed on schedule. The trip qualifies as a once-in-a-lifetime experience. It is a giant journey which makes most other train rides seem like a trip around the block. Travelers accustomed to jets might object to the six days of travel covering 4,700 miles, roughly equivalent to going from New York City to Phoenix and back again. The trip is an interdisciplinary short course, a curving train of subject matter. It is not a vacation. Who, after all, would take a vacation that includes five nights of cramped sleeping, gritty soot from steam engines, washrooms designed for contortionists, irregular eating, enough time zones to confound most bodily functions, and a lifetime supply of jostling and jerking.

The planning of the trip had begun months earlier and seemed problematic for some time, since we were traveling independently rather than with a tour group, which gets priority treatment in China. Travelers on organized tours, of course, pay more than do independent travelers. We first had to decide which Trans-Siberian route to take out of Beijing: through Manchuria, the route of the Russian train, or through Mongolia, the route of the Chinese train. Costs and travel time for the two routes were about the same. The Chinese train, we were told, is cleaner and the food better. We found the Chinese train to be clean, but the food we could not judge. Incredibly, in six days we never had a meal in the dining car, because it was closed or serving only group tours or something else. We had anticipated such a problem and had loaded up on provisions in Beijing. Our luggage at the outset consisted of nine pieces, and the contents of three were consumed in travel.

To stave off boredom, we had also stored up reading matter. If we

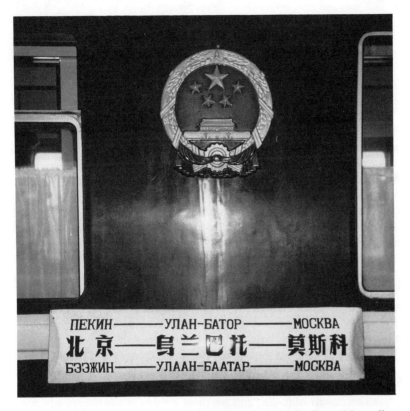

A SIGN on a car of the Trans-Mongolian
International Express Train tells the route
in Russian, Chinese, and Mongolian:
Beijing-Ulan Bator-Moscow.

had planned more carefully, we would have taken along a copy of
Robert Strauss's informative *Trans-Siberian Rail Guide* (1987) and
maybe Eric Newby's enjoyable *The Big Red Train Ride* (1978).

The Chinese train offers a choice of three classes of ticket: first
class (also called deluxe), soft sleeper, and hard sleeper. All are comfortable, offering better accommodations—including Western-style
toilets—than most domestic Chinese trains. Most expensive is first
class. Travel agents snap up these tickets before independent travelers
can get a chance at them. First-class compartments have two beds and
have shower facilities between every two compartments. The cost is

1016.90 *yuan* ($274.84 U.S.). We had the soft sleeper. Each unit has four berths to a compartment. The fourth berth in our unit was unoccupied, which was fortuitous, given the amount of our luggage. The cost for each of us was 890.70 *yuan* ($240.73 U.S.). The trains run this route once a week.

Acquiring tickets and visas also required careful planning. If it had not been for a Chinese friend who negotiated the intricate bureaucracy of the China International Travel Service (CITS), I do not think we would have obtained tickets. Reservations could not be made more than one month in advance of scheduled departure. Visas had to be obtained in reverse order of travel, that is, starting with the final destination and working back. We already had Chinese visas. We had to get Soviet visas through the Soviet Embassy in Beijing and book accommodations for the Soviet Union through Intourist at outrageous prices — per night $150 U.S. for three persons in one room in Moscow and $180 U.S. in Leningrad.

Shortly out of Beijing, our steward, Zhao Wenqing, brought sheets and towels. He also brought a hot-water thermos, the omnipresence of which signals the civilized nature of the Chinese people. Mr. Zhao, age forty-one, worked hard keeping the compartments clean, his tenants satisfied, and his uniform neat. He obviously enjoyed his job. The father of two, he makes eight to ten round-trips a year between Beijing and Moscow. In seventeen years, he said, he had made the trip nearly 170 times.

The countryside east and north of Beijing is a lush green in midsummer. When we had seen it last, on our early January trip to the steam-engine locomotive city of Datong, the land was drab and brown with patches of snow. Now cornfields abounded. The green foliage soon gave way to hills of brown earth, as entire villages constructed of brown mud bricks rose out of the countryside. The train stopped a few minutes in Datong to pick up a dozen members of a travel group from Belgium. North, the land became flatter, dryer. Rolling grasslands emerged, along with horses, sheep, goats, and, occasionally, camels and cranes. Watching the changing landscape flicker by became a major pastime for us.

At 8:34 p.m. we rolled into Erlian, the last stop in China and the longest of the entire trip at two hours, thirty-nine minutes. Here the bogies (wheel carriages) on the train were changed to fit the wider Russian track (1,524 mm as compared to the Chinese gauge of 1,435 mm). During the wait on the train platform, a loudspeaker blared

ZHAO WENQING, steward on the
Trans-Mongolian International Express

"Roll Out the Barrel" and Strauss waltzes. Near midnight, we stopped
at the border of Outer Mongolia.

From the windows we saw eerie shadows. They were guards with
rifles. Customs officials boarded and instructed us to complete "customs declaration" forms. This struck us as comic since we would not
really spend any time in Outer Mongolia. Nor did we have any "raw
foodstuffs of animal origin." But we did not laugh, for there were
shadows in the night. It was past midnight by the time the train began
moving again.

We awoke early the morning of the second day to see plains

sprawling endlessly in all directions. Herders on horseback were tending sheep and goats. Nearby were their nomadic homes, *yurts*. Visible everywhere were Soviet soldiers and military trucks, mobile radar units, and jet fighters, a reminder of tensions between China and the Soviet Union. Outer Mongolia has been tucked in the Soviet orbit, a buffer region for the USSR.

Shortly after noon we arrived in Ulan Bator (Red Hero), the capital of Outer Mongolia with a population of about three hundred thousand. We walked around the station, which was nearly vacant, glanced into several kiosks, snapped a few photographs, and then rushed back to the train. The stop was for ten minutes. Our lives soon were to revolve around these ten-minute intervals, which offered the opportunity to stretch muscles, to experience something different from the monotony of the train, and, simply, to be able to say with modest authority, assuming anyone else would be interested, that we had been to these exotic places.

About 11 p.m. we made our last stop in Mongolia, the town of Sühbaatar. Customs officials went back to work. A young, uniformed soldier eyed our forms and glanced at a two-month-old issue of the *New York Times Sunday Magazine* that I had borrowed from a Canadian journalist who was on the train. The soldier riveted his attention on our nineteen-year-old daughter's musical audio tapes. He sorted through the dozen titles and pulled out one. He adjusted the earphones, listening intently for several minutes. We could be in trouble. Suddenly a smile emerged. He winked and flashed a thumbs-up sign. We had passed. So had the Eurythmics.

The train resumed but stopped again after ten minutes. Now it was a border check by the Soviets. From past experience, I knew they could be tough, going through every bag. A customs official, a stout, stern woman, asked us for our visas and wrote our names in her ledger. That was all. Because it was late or because of *glasnost*-induced hospitality or whatever, she cleared us quickly and suggested we might want to change money. That was the reason for the cursory check — to make sure there was time to change money. I asked the woman who had written down our names if we would have any trouble finding an Intourist official once we arrived in Moscow. She said emphatically, "Intourist will find you." I believed her.

THE TRAIN STATION in Ulan Bator

Early Friday morning we got off the train to stretch our legs at the USSR-Mongolian border town of Naüshki. Siberia lay ahead. Time was beginning to get muddled. Until now we had been on the same time as Beijing. From now on, all official train times were to be given according to the Moscow time zone. This sounds simple enough except that the USSR has eleven different time zones including Moscow's. Presumably, the trip still takes six days.

The landscape flitting past had changed again. Now we were in a mountainous area with lots of birch and pine trees and streams and ponds. Out one window we saw hay being cut by hand. Out the opposite window across the aisle was a lake. It was Lake Baikal (meaning "rich lake"), the world's deepest. The crystal clear water is a mile deep in places. The lake is nearly four hundred miles long and covers an area equal to the Netherlands and Belgium combined. Two-thirds of the five hundred plants and twelve hundred animals found in and around the lake are not found anywhere else.

Our first disembarking point in the Soviet Union was at Slyud-yanka along the southern part of the lake. It turned out to be a Siberian oasis for us. Old Russian women, called *babushkas,* had set up an open market along the tracks and were selling fresh vegetables and berries. We managed to buy carrots and strawberries before the train resumed its relentless march.

Several hours later we pulled into Irkutsk, the so-called Paris of Siberia, a title earned through trading tea and gold. Now the regional center of Eastern Siberia, it was originally a winter camp for the cossacks in 1652. In 1985 a third of the city's population consisted of exiles. In fact, much of the construction of the Trans-Siberian Railway, which runs 5,776 miles from Moscow to Vladivostok, was done by exiles and convicts. If they did a satisfactory job, they got their sentences reduced by a third. But the construction, which took place from 1891 to 1915, was not without danger. Accidents and illness claimed thousands of lives. In one stretch around Lake Baikal, 368 deaths were recorded for each *verst* (about one-seventh of a mile). The Trans-Siberian line, Russia's "main street," represented an important political and military link for the Soviet Union. It was not until January 1, 1956, that the Beijing-Mongolia linkup opened to traffic.

Siberia's land mass is staggering. It is nearly one and one-half times the size of the fifty United States. Rich with natural resources, the region has always exuded raw potential, little of which has been realized. From the train, Siberia seems luxuriant and inviting. It ap-

RUSSIAN *BABUSHKAS* sell fresh vegetables and berries to train travelers.

pears to be a good place to visit for the summer, but I would want a return ticket in hand.

About 2:30 in the afternoon, we pulled into the Zima Station, the twenty-sixth stop on this marathon journey. This pause was to be for fifteen minutes. Again, the *babushkas,* their hair tucked beneath brightly colored scarves, lined the tracks waiting for hungry train travelers. We bought blueberries, boiled fresh potatoes, and dill pickles. Although Siberia looked green and inviting this time of year, it was still Siberia, and we did not stray far from the train. Unknown to us at the time, one of the occupants of our car, Klaus, a university student from West Germany, failed to return. The train left without him. Of course, no one knew it at the time. Nearly eight hours passed, taking us through Tulun, Nizhneudinsk, and Hanskaya, before Klaus's compartment mates, also from West Germany, confirmed what they had suspected hours earlier after searching all seventeen cars: Klaus was stranded in Siberia.

For everyone except poor Klaus, the incident evoked dark humor. Someone adapted an old joke and said that now Klaus could do whatever he wanted because there was nothing more anyone could do to him—he already was in Siberia. Klaus's misfortune did serve as one of the more interesting interludes in the routine of a trip that was beginning to border on forever. The next day, at Achinsk, Soviet authorities boarded the train. Klaus's friend, Peter, left with them. He was to wait for Klaus who was on a domestic train three hours behind ours. The two then would complete the trip together. We never saw or heard about them again. For us, Klaus and Peter will be stranded forever in one of those small, unresolved mysteries of life.

Our fellow passengers were mostly Westerners. There were several Canadians, a few Americans, including four college students who had been teaching in South Korea, and a handful of others who had spent the year teaching in China. Besides the Belgian tour group, there were quite a few young people from Europe. Apart from the train crew, there was only one Chinese passenger. Yang Zongkun of Wuhan in Hubei Province was traveling to Warsaw to attend an Esperanto Congress. He was thrilled by the trip. He said he could not afford it himself but that the Polish hosts were providing funds.

The tree-covered hills continued to roll by endlessly. Wood is winter's lifeline here, and stacks of it dotted the countryside, often occupying more space than the drab wooden houses with their colorful shutters.

On the early morning of the fourth day, we stopped at Krasnoyarsk. At this and every other crossing, old men or women—crossing guards—stood at attention, resolutely holding a colored flag or sign with a number. In early evening we were at Novosibirsk, the "Chicago of Siberia," so called because it is a major port city on the River Ob. It is the largest city in the region with a population of about 1.5 million. We gave it fifteen minutes. It was dark by the time we got to Omsk, where in the middle 1800s Fyodor Dostoyevski spent four years in exile, writing *Recollections of a Dead House* (also translated as *Buried in Siberia*). The stops now were beginning to become blurred. Disorientation was setting in. We were now in an endurance test.

On the fifth day, the Siberian sunrise was spectacular. A fog rose slowly over the low-lying, swamplike landscape. Or was it a moonscape? Were creatures at this moment stirring to life out there in those mists?

One way to mark the journey is by the architecture of Siberia's railway stations. Unfortunately that too became boring. Most of the stations were large, rectangular, fortresslike structures. Stations in the smaller towns had more character. They were made of wood and were about the size of large houses. The Zima Station, where Klaus was left behind, easily captured first place in our informal competition. It was all wood with decorative windows and roof angles that suggested it should be in a fairy tale. Dotting the countryside were wooden houses with gingerbread fronts.

Midmorning. Another fifteen-minute stop: Sverdlovsk, the Pittsburgh of the Urals. Here in 1960 American pilot Gary Powers was brought down in a U-2 reconnaissance plane. About an hour outside the city is a stone obelisk into which is etched in Russian the word *Asia* on one side and *Europe* on the other. A train passing ours in the opposite direction prevented us from seeing the marker.

Our supply of food and reading material was running low. Not exactly life threatening. Merely a minor concern. And on this Sunday, a special treat awaited. The Canadian journalist had brought a copy of the *Sunday Times of London*. No matter that it was dated the previous Sunday. The last stop of the day was the industrial city of Kirov.

The sixth day did not come too soon, although, oddly, by now we felt as though we were in a race that could end in a photo finish. Because of lost time at border checkpoints, the crew was hurrying to make up the time. Stops became shorter and shorter. No matter how short, though, we managed to recover only a few of the lost minutes. We were in a cocoon hurtling across time and space, neither of which seemed to matter anymore. Early morning found us at the Danilov Station, where to our delight the now familiar *babushkas* were hawking fresh berries.

About 8 a.m. we made our last stop before Moscow at Yaroslavl. It is the oldest town on the Volga River, tracing its written history to 1071. Here a massive bridge spans the Volga, the longest river in Europe, flowing more than twenty-two hundred miles to the Caspian Sea.

At 18 minutes past noon Moscow time, our train eased to a final stop at Moscow's Yaroslavl Station. It was our forty-eighth stop. We were 33 minutes late. It had taken 129 hours and 38 minutes to travel from Beijing to Moscow.

EPILOGUE

Two years—a millennium, it seems— have passed since our return to the States. My thoughts often turn to China. I think of the rich Chinese culture we were privileged to experience, of the changes that have taken place, of the hopes that those changes sustain, and of the students and their families. And of Tiananmen Square, where, despite a cultural propensity to humility, Chinese come to take photos and express a hint of pride in country and accomplishment. We still remember Tiananmen Square on China's National Day, decorated in floral splendor, resembling a pendant in a necklace of resplendent fall colors. Now we think of June 4, 1989, and of the makeshift bicycle ambulances and the eerie nighttime flashes across the television screen as gunfire and chaos and death invaded China's national shrine.

I reflect on the difficulty of coping with another culture, of struggling to see another culture by looking from the inside out rather than by looking from the outside in. China scholar John King Fairbank has framed the issue nicely: "How from outside a foreign culture can one reach large conclusions without jumping to them?" (1986, p. 358). Performing such perceptual leapfrog is, of course, difficult if not impossible. Yet it is an effort that people must make if they expect tolerance, respect, and peace in the world.

Vivid in my mind is that August evening when we arrived in China at the Beijing International Airport. Confusion reigned. Soon the unsettledness turned to acceptance and coping. It became perfectly ordinary to go to the China airlines and arrange a trip one-way because that was the only way we could arrange it ourselves. There was nothing unusual about enthusiastically looking forward to a Sunday, along with millions of others for whom this was their only day during the week away from work.

221

What was unusual after the year was returning to the States and being confronted by a society that seemed to totter on the edge of schizophrenia. Time and space became jumbled. The abundance and diversity were numbing at every turn, whether it was the media or the supermarket. Or had they become the same? Life at home was complex — and this after we had become accustomed in China to taking off half a day to do banking and to spending hours simply mailing a box of books to a friend in Nanjing.

One year in China was not enough time to experience the country or to develop much competency in the language. But it was long enough to begin appreciating a culture vastly different from our own. My family and I came to realize that we knew even less than we had suspected. An American journalism teacher who has taught in China several years commented to me that he had been in China too long to write a book. The more he learned, the more complex things got. Such is the way of trying to understand things.

And what of the changes we witnessed in China? Is China really changing? Many of my friends, including experts on China as well as Chinese themselves, say no: "The more things change in China, the more they remain the same."

One writer discussing change in China put it this way: "Great allowance must therefore be made for the difficult position in which Chinese statesmen find themselves. Reforms they know to be necessary; but their duty is so to temper them that they may be adopted with the least possible shock to indigenous institutions" (p. 369). That was written more than a century ago — in 1864 — by an Englishman, Alexander Michie, in a fascinating account of an overland trip from Beijing to St. Petersburg (now Leningrad). The observation is ominously similar to the Communist party line in defending the 1989 military crackdown.

News items with Beijing datelines keep intruding: "Americans warned of terrorist threat" is one headline. The article tells of warnings to the fifteen hundred Americans in Beijing about becoming possible targets of terrorist attacks. This is startling. Security and surveillance make China one of the safest places in the world for a foreigner. Kentucky Fried Chicken opens a restaurant just south of Tiananmen Square. A new ambassador is appointed to China. And what is this story about the thirty-four-year-old farmer, Liu Xigui of Shenyang, Liaoning Province, who has accumulated assets worth more than 5.2 million *yuan* ($1.4 million U.S.)? He wants to join the Communist party. Talk about contradictions!

May 1989. Now come the student demonstrations. Spirits soar as high as the kites that often flutter above Tiananmen Square. Change triggers change. Will China seize the historic moment? The answers ring out with bursts of gunfire, and there is bedlam. There is the news of Mark Hopkins, the VOA newsman who visited my class. He is accused of violating provisions of martial law and is expelled from China. There is Wang Meng, the novelist who spoke to us foreign experts about the resurgence of artistic freedom. Wang Meng, who helped my student win the appellation "Scoop," is dismissed as the nation's Culture Minister. Still more restrictions are placed on students wanting to study abroad. Even the English language corner in Beijing's Purple Bamboo Park is closed down. Robust talk about increasing press freedom now seems like an echo from China's distant past. The fate of Hong Kong and its residents becomes more perilous.

China, indeed, always has experienced change. But then change occurs naturally in every life form. It is the nature of the change in China that is unpredictable and often inexplicable. When we were there, change was in the direction of greater responsiveness to people and improvement in the standard of living. In the aftermath of June 1989, the change is regressive and brutal. Yet during the 1980s powerful economic forces were unleashed. The door to the world was opened. Chinese leaders themselves admit there is no turning back. There is the difficult matter of orchestrating the change. Officials say stability is necessary for continued development, but they are equally adamant about holding on to power. There is much room for abuse and errors in this process. In such circumstances, it is possible for the central government to justify nearly any kind of action. But governments, as is evident in Eastern Europe, can change. In the end, it is the people who will prevail, and the same one day will happen for the people of the world's most populous nation ironically called the People's Republic.

And the students. What of the students? *My* students. One writes:

> Dear professor: Since you worked in the country for quite a long time, I guess that you understand my generation more than your compatriots. Things are getting worse and worse since the government's crackdown on the pro-democratic movement. . . . Ideological control has been tightened. . . . We are a generation of responsibility. We labored, suffered and were deprived of study opportunities during the "cultural revolution" over ten years ago. We were no longer young when the nation's nightmare ended.

Thus, we dared not idle one moment away. . . . For a decade, we
have been working hard in an attempt to make up for the time lost.
Although disillusioned, we still hold aspirations and goals, that is,
leading a meaningful life and working for a better, prosperous
China.

The students and I stay in touch. Since many are part of the
government communication apparatus, they must be careful. This
means keeping in check their feelings and some of their ideas, or else
they could jeopardize promising and coveted careers enabling them to
travel fairly freely and maybe even abroad. Some have become dis-
couraged. Three have come to the United States to study. One of
them, among the most gifted in the class, became disenchanted with
the work unit, left the program, and is now studying a subject related
to business. The other two won awards to continue studying journalism. At least three others have left their work units and are desper-
ately seeking opportunities to study abroad. Others are settling into
their positions, dedicated to doing their part in helping build the new
China.

Again, from my student's letter: "Although we are under the
reign of terror and do not enjoy any freedom of speech and expression, we are not intimidated, and feel confident that such a reac-
tionary and unpopular rule is not to last very long."

My student is generous in suggesting I understand the student's
generation. At least I think I understand the difference between people as human beings and people in a collective sense under control of
a political machine. But I do not understand events in China. Even
Chinese essayist Lu Xun wondered more than fifty years ago why it is
that in China the old write the obituaries of the young rather than the
other way around.

The students and I have a date. Early in the academic year we
spent together I mentioned that I would eagerly be following their
careers.

"Maybe in the year 2000," I offhandedly commented one day, "we
can get together and find out what's been happening to each of us."

They liked the idea. We agreed informally to meet for a reunion
in the year 2000.

SELECTED REFERENCES

Avedon, John F. 1986. *In Exile from the Land of Snows*. New York: Vintage Books.

Barlow, Tani E., and Donald M. Lowe. 1987. *Teaching China's Lost Generation: Foreign Experts in the People's Republic of China*. San Francisco: China Books & Periodicals, first published as *Chinese Reflections*.

Barmé, Geremie, and John Minford, eds. 1986. *Seeds of Fire: Chinese Voices of Conscience*. Hong Kong: Far Eastern Economic Review.

Bonavia, David. 1982. *The Chinese*. Middlesex, Eng.: Penguin; Pelican rev. ed.

Buckley, Michael, and Robert Strauss. 1986. *Tibet—A Travel Survival Kit*. Berkeley: Lonely Planet.

Butterfield, Fox. 1983. *China: Alive in the Bitter Sea*. Toronto: Bantam Books; Times Book ed., 1982.

Cai Xiqin. 1986. *A Visit to Confucius' Home Town*. Trans. by Rosemary A. Roberts. Beijing: New World Press.

Chen Yong, *et al.*, eds. 1988. *The Great Tangshan Earthquake of 1976: An Anatomy of Disaster*. Oxford: Pergamon Press.

Clayre, Alasdair. 1985. *The Heart of the Dragon*. Boston: Houghton Mifflin.

Dietrich, Craig. 1986. *People's China: A Brief History*. New York: Oxford.

Fairbank, John King. 1986. *The Great Chinese Revolution: 1800–1985*. New York: Harper & Row.

——. 1987. *China Watch*. Cambridge: Harvard University Press.

Gao Yuan. 1987. *Born Red: A Chronicle of the Cultural Revolution*. Stanford: Stanford University Press.

Hamilton, John Maxwell. 1988. *Edgar Snow: A Biography*. Bloomington and Indianapolis: Indiana University Press.

Harrer, Heinrich. 1983. *Return to Tibet*. Trans. by Ewald Osers. Middlesex, Eng.: Penguin.

Hersey, John. 1986. *The Call*. New York: Penguin.

Jenner, Delia. 1967. *Letters from Peking*. London: Oxford University Press.

Latsch, Marie-Luise. 1984. *Chinese Traditional Festivals*. Beijing: New World Press.

Liang Heng, and Judith Shapiro. 1984. *Son of the Revolution.* New York: Vintage.

Liu Zongren. 1984. *Two Years in the Melting Pot.* San Francisco: China Books & Periodicals.

MacKinnon, Stephen R., and Oris Friesen. 1987. *China Reporting: An Oral History of American Journalism in the 1930s and 1940s.* Berkeley: University of California Press.

Mathews, Jay, and Linda Mathews. 1983. *One Billion: A China Chronicle.* New York: Random House.

Michie, Alexander. 1864. *The Siberian Overland Route from Peking to Petersburg, through the Deserts and Steppes of Mongolia, Tartary, &c.* London: John Murray, Albermarle Street.

Morton, W. Scott. 1982. *China: Its History and Culture.* New York: McGraw-Hill.

Mosher, Steven W. 1983. *Broken Earth: The Rural Chinese.* New York: The Free Press.

Needham, Joseph. 1981. *Science in Traditional China: A Comparative Perspective.* Cambridge: Harvard University Press.

Newby, Eric. 1980. *The Big Red Train Ride.* Middlesex, Eng.: Penguin; originally St. Martin's Press.

O'Neill, Hugh B. 1987. *Companion to Chinese History.* New York: Facts on File Publications.

Salisbury, Harrison. 1987. *The Long March: The Untold Story.* New York: McGraw-Hill Book Company.

Salzman, Mark. 1987. *Iron & Silk.* New York: Random House, Vintage ed.

Samagalski, Alan, Michael Buckley, and Robert Strauss. 1988. *China—A Travel Survival Kit.* 2d ed. Berkeley: Lonely Planet.

Schell, Orville. 1986. *To Get Rich Is Glorious: China in the 80s.* New York: Mentor.

———. 1988. *Discos and Democracy: China in the Throes of Reform.* New York: Pantheon Books.

Snellgrove, David, and Hugh Richardson. 1986. *A Cultural History of Tibet.* Boston & London: Shambhala.

Snow, Edgar. 1978. *Red Star Over China.* New York: Bantam Books; originally Random House, 1938.

Spence, Jonathan D. 1981. *The Gate of Heavenly Peace: The Chinese and Their Revolution 1895–1980.* Middlesex, Eng.: Penguin Books.

———. 1988. *The Question of Hu.* New York: Vintage Books.

Strauss, Robert. 1987. *Trans-Siberian Rail Guide.* Bucks, Eng.: Bradt Publications; distributed in the United States by Hunter Publishing, Inc., Edison, N.J.

Sullivan, Michael. 1984. *The Arts of China.* 3d ed. Berkeley: University of California Press.

Terzani, Tiziano. 1987. *Behind the Forbidden Door: China Inside Out*. Hong Kong: ASIA 2000.

Theroux, Paul. 1975. *The Great Railway Bazaar: By Train through Asia*. New York: Houghton Mifflin.

_____. 1988. *Riding the Iron Rooster: By Train through China*. New York: G. P. Putnam's Sons.

Tupper, Harmon. 1965. *To the Great Ocean; Siberia and the Trans-Siberian Railway*. Boston: Little, Brown & Company.

Turner-Gottschang, Karen, with Linda A. Reed. 1987. *China Bound: A Guide to Academic Life and Work in the PRC*. Washington, D.C.: National Academy Press.

Wilby, Sorrel. 1988. *Journey Across Tibet: A Young Woman's 1900-Mile Trek Across the Rooftop of the World*. Chicago: Contemporary Books.

INDEX